Praise for Happy Woman Magazine:

"Devilish wit" —USA Today

"A welcome oasis" —The Globe and Mail

"With satire like this, who needs mascara?" —Yahoo Internet Life Magazine, Best and Worst Issue

"Politely vicious satire" —The Vancouver Sun

Random Acts of Malice

The Best of HAPPY WOMAN MAGAZINE

Edited by Sharon Grehan

Featuring work by the some of the best satirists on the planet:

Sharon Grehan, Elizabeth Hanes, Elaine Langlois, Pamela Monk, Jessica Becht, Mike Boone, Crystal Click, Christina Delia, Stephen James, Meredith Litt, Susan Shoemaker, Diane Sokoloski, Sarah Szucs, and Julie Ward...

Can you afford NOT to buy this book?

Random Acts of Malice: The Best of Happy Woman Magazine
Edited by Sharon Grehan
isbn 1-894953-32-0
www.happywomanmagazine.com
Liaison Press
First edition – November 2005
CGP-4005

Published in Canada by Liaison Press, an imprint of Creative Guy Publishing
Vancouver, BC, Canada
www.creativeguypublishing.com / www.liaisonpress.com

Random Acts of Malice

The Best of HAPPY WOMAN MAGAZINE

Edited by Sharon Grehan

L I A I S O N   P R E S S
VANCOUVER · BRITISH COLUMBIA · CANADA

Random Acts of Malice

The Best of HAPPY WOMAN MAGAZINE

Edited by Sharon Grehan

L I A I S O N P R E S S
VANCOUVER · BRITISH COLUMBIA · CANADA

Message from Above

Congratulations on your very fine judgment! *The Best of Happy Woman Magazine* is just what the title suggests — the very best of the award winning website Happy Woman Magazine.com. Inside you will find miles and miles — well, actually if each page is laid end to end you will have approximately 2914 inches of humour, which is a lot.

To all of the people who have slaved away for the past five years making Happy Woman Magazine the blazing success that it is (you know who you are!) without a word of thanks or praise, and to all the loyal readers and fans, I would like to take this opportunity to say "You're welcome!"

Sharon Grehan
Editor
Much Beloved Founder

Table of Contents

Chapter Six – June

Chapter Seven – July

Chapter Eight – August

Chapter Nine – September

TABLE OF CONTENTS

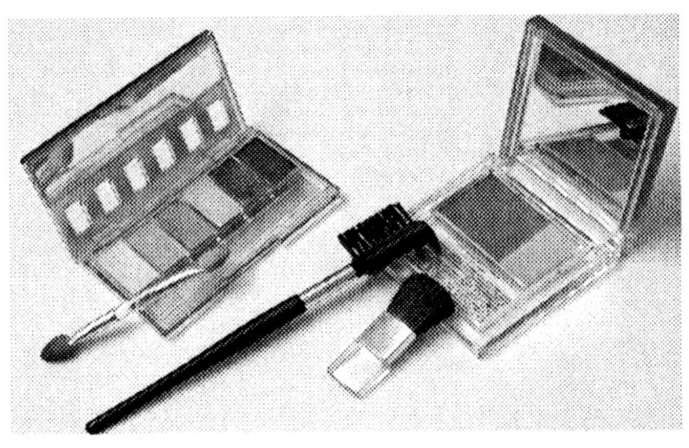

Chapter Ten – October

Chapter Eleven – November

Chapter Twelve – December

Chapter One – January

Letters to the Editor

By Meredith Litt

Life is a Highway

AS A DRIVER of a mid-size SUV, I wanted to applaud you for "Women Take the Power Back, Highway-Style," your breathtaking article in April. After centuries of oppression by the male race, we have finally been given the keys to the pearly gates, complete with air conditioning and dual airbags. All of these right-wing zealots assert that many females who drive minivans and SUVs are aggressive. Well, why shouldn't we be? Cutting off some macho man or passing a father of four in a no-pass zone is nothing compared to the eons we spent bearing their children and being forced to let them provide for us financially. Kudos to you for empowering women everywhere to unleash years of pent-up frustration on America's highways. I've just renewed my subscription for another year and taken my Nissan Pathfinder in for neon lights.
—Jaime, Tennessee.

Bullies Bite Back

I read "I Was Bullied in High School" (May 2004) and was appalled by how you portrayed the "in crowds" in America's high schools. Like it or not, we are the way of the future. Having spent my entire life at only the elite lunch tables of this world, I was appalled that your magazine (one that prides itself on virtues of fashion, vanity, and extrinsic beauty) would glorify the "plight" of the pond's ugliest duckling. All the girl had to do was ride her bike over to the drugstore and invest in some Maybelline stock. I'm tired of magazines glorifying the ugly women of this world and trying to make those of us who spend hours on our appearance feel inferior. It's this kind of oppression that keeps womankind at bay in the working world. As a wise woman (me) once said, "One ugly duckling contaminates the entire pond." Shame on you for selling out and catering to the fashion proletariat.
—Kerri, Michigan.

Reading "I Was Bullied in High School" made me remember my high school days with sadness. I was tortured in high school to the point of tears (oh, how I envy those popular girls who never had reason to be sad about anything) because I refused to bathe. I felt as if bathing was pointless: why wash it off when, the next day, another layer of dirt would be there to replace it? It's not like I was endangering the public with toxic fumes; it was just some natural body odour. Thank you for showing me that I wasn't the only teenager who has ever been depressed. I thought that I was the only angsty adolescent in the history of the world.
—Penelope, via Internet.

Matrimonial Bliss

Thank you, thank you, thank you for your feature on how to plan your very own celebrity wedding (May 2004). All of the bridal magazines I've read have been so run-of-the-mill, so imagine my joy when I found weddings featured in your magazine that were in my elevated price range. After seeing the success of celebrity marriages, I am convinced that the more expensive the wedding, the longer the marriage will last.

My parents eloped at city hall the day after my mom learned she was pregnant with me, and their marriage lasted five years. What more proof do you need? While brides across America are chowing down on buttercream icing, I'll be enjoying my 24K gold glazed saffron cake. I am so glad that there is a magazine out there with enough class to showcase REAL weddings instead of the bourgeois parties girls these days are throwing.
—Jenna, Maryland.

Note from the editor:
Thank you for writing, Jenna. We, too, thought that today's pedestrian weddings are too heavily featured in today's magazines. It is only fair that we shed equal light on ceremonies that cost upward of $1,000,000. If we cater to the poor, we must also cater to the rich. Look for more features in the future on upper-class wedding rituals and more fabulous diamond-encrusted gowns from the world's most treasured designers. That's what the wedding is all about, after all! •*HW*•

Corrections
By Julie Ward

WE APOLOGIZE for the recent *Careers* feature, "New Opportunities for Pear-Shaped Models." As soon as we published it, the author phoned to say she had submitted it for the *Fiction* section, or perhaps the *Twisted Humour Corner.* We did not want to shatter our beloved readers' dreams without checking a few facts first, so we called our sources in the fashion industry and asked, "What is the outlook for the pear-shaped modelling business?" Immediately after our sources stopped laughing and saying, "Good joke," we learned that there are no jobs in fashion for pear-shaped models, and there never have been—not even part time, temporary, pro bono or itinerant. We encourage all of our lovely-on-the-inside, bottom-heavy readers to pursue a more realistic career goal, such as pear-shaped neurosurgeon or pear-shaped rocket scientist.

Our *Parenting* story, "Is Your Child Perfect or Are You Just Obnoxious—Five Ways to Tell," quoted child rearing expert Dr. Robert Fleester. Unfortunately, we recently discovered that Dr. Fleester has not been allowed to practice clinical psychology since the early 1990s because of his irresponsible use of sarcasm and sadism when treating the chronically literal-minded (CLM). This information casts new light on Dr. Fleester's "advice," and we now believe that he was being sarcastic rather than helpful when he said,

"Your friends and family really want to hear about your perfect child. Really. They really really do. All the time, in fact. So go ahead and tell them every little thing that your child does oh-so-perfectly, in the most minute detail. Better yet, put it in a blog so the whole world can see." We asked a different child rearing expert, one who has not yet brought shame to the profession, to re-evaluate the conclusions of our article. She is pretty sure your child isn't perfect, and almost certain that you *are* annoying. We regret any inconvenience this has caused you, such as a false sense of well-being, and/or bewilderment about why the other parents seem to be blocking your phone calls. Rest assured our next "Multitasking Mama" column was written with you in mind—we'll help you work on that annoying personality while you trim your thighs!

In the *Medical Advice* column, Dr. Ramses Sesram told the letter writer that he doubted if medication was helping and that she should feel free to discontinue it. Unfortunately, Dr. Sesram meant to type "meditation" instead of "medication." He urges the letter writer, as well as all the lovely psychotic readers in our publication's extended family, to continue to take their psychiatrist-prescribed medication—if it's not too late.

In the *Cooking* section, many readers wrote in to complain about our recipe for Gingerbread Friends. Apparently, if you follow step 3 ("Use cinnamon massage oil and rub vigorously"), your Gingerbread Friends turn out uncharacteristically spicy and stiff. We apologize for this breach of trust in our usually dependable relationship. We understand that you rely on us to provide recipes that are delicious and do not remind you of a French whorehouse while you are baking. The Cooking editor has asked us to assure you that she "got this recipe confused with a little something something that you really don't need to concern yourself with," and that it probably won't happen again.

In our featured *Craft*, the instructions for crocheting your own fishnet hose in spring's fabulous new colours should have ended but didn't. In reply to our many dear but sarcastic readers, No, we don't know whether the Jolly Green Giant needs a new pair of fishnets. But not to worry, fashionistas—our travel editor reports that fishnet overalls have been spotted this week in Monte Carlo, Miami Beach, Ipanema, and on one runway in New York (well, to be truthful, it was a private airstrip on Staten Island). We humbly ask our dear, disgruntled, crafting readers to make a serious attempt to repurpose their fishnets before their attorneys contact us again. •*HW*•

QUIZ—Have You Been on a Date?

Take our quiz and find out!

By Stephen James

IN THE 1950'S it was easy to tell if you had been on a date. If you were a boy, you had lipstick on your collar and felt like you'd scored the winning goal, only better. If you were a girl, you had a crumpled pinafore and thoughts about what colour he will decorate the nursery when you're married.

Nowadays, relationships between and even within the sexes are more complicated. We live in a world of post-modern rainbow sexuality in which everything is fluid and provisional. In many ways things are better now, especially for the girls who used to put lipstick on the collars of boys who would rather be riding bareback with John Wayne; and for the boys who used to crumple the pinafores of girls who would rather be out crumpling some other girl's pinafore.

So if you have just spent some time with a person but are not sure if it was a date, try this quick fire quiz to find out.

1. How are you acquainted with your companion?

a. We met through a reputable introduction agency. No, really.

b. We are colleagues writing a joint Ph.D. on sexuality and power in the workplace.

c. S/he is just a random boy/girl who turns up.

2. How would you describe your companion's body language?

a. Lots of inappropriate hand-shakes, strange moans and queer looks.

b. Shaking slightly, with a wild and anxious eye, until given some drugs. Then, catatonic.

c. Suave and debonair with plenty of flourishes, like a Fred Astaire movie.

3. Which university degree best describes your sexual dynamics with this person?

a. Chemistry

b. Biology

c. Psychology

d. Media/Gender Studies

4. How would you rate the formality of the occasion?

a. We read through the minutes of the previous meeting before getting started.

b. He/she brought along various pets and children in case we got bored.

c. He/she no longer leaves my bed in order to break wind.

5. How would you describe your companion's role in the sexual team?

a. Ideas person

b. Completer-finisher

c. Corporate worker

d. Chairman

Next step: pick a number of points corresponding to the answer you want to have. Then read the answers.

0-10 points. You were not on a date. You were in fact at a departmental meeting. You were rather taken with the look of a colleague whom you have not noticed in that way before. Your mind wandered off and you had a rather pleasant fantasy. You had agreed to give a presentation, but after saying your name twice without response the chair-person moved on to discuss the forthcoming Directorate Away-Day.

11-20 points. You are very much in demand, not to say needed. You've let your companion pay for your cup of coffee and s/he now believes that you are twin souls knit into one. S/he will be upset if you ever go anywhere without him/her for any reason at all. Consequently your job may be at risk, and visits to the toilet will be irksome. It is best to gently extricate yourself now while the going is good.

21-30 points. You have just been on a post-modern date in which everything is an ironic pastiche of an out-dated dating culture. You haven't been on a date, you've been on a "date." Some people think this is a sophisticated way of going on, others think it is just a defense mechanism against possible sexual rejection. Some people live their entire lives this way. After "dating," they "get married" and "have a family." Post-modernism is no longer in its infancy, and it is increasingly common to meet the offspring of such unions who say things like, "I'm going 'on holiday' next month with 'the parents'." Meanwhile, the parents have found that although putting quotation marks round things may be a way of life, it does not amount to a philosophy. But that's another story.

31-40 points. You've been on a "pre-date." This is a practice run for a date. When adults pre-date, their motivation is often a desire to generate sexual excitement without the risk of failure, rejection or fulfillment.
Pre-dating is fun in itself and can become a way of life, but many people find they want a bit more after a while.

Over 40 points. You have just been on a date. It is 1956. Your pinafore is slightly crumpled and your cheeks are flushed. You want to ring up your best friend but it is already 11.45 and you are afraid of waking your Mum. You can still hear his voice, feel his breath on your cheek and smell his jacket. You can't believe he chose you out of all the girls. No-one has ever felt this happy in the history of the world. The beautiful thing is, you know he feels exactly the same way. You wonder if his parents will ask him about the lipstick on his collar and if they do what he will say about you.

You think about houses. Then about cribs. Then about the funny way he laughs, with a little scream at the end. Why does he do that? And why does he have pictures of John Wayne all over the dashboard? You will not sleep tonight. And you know that he will be awake too. •*HW*•

The Alphabet Diet—As simple as A-B-C!
By Sharon Grehan

THIS REVOLUTIONARY and exclusive diet based on the sound science of Alphadietics is guaranteed to work! After weeks of searching, the HW scientists discovered that all foods from A-Z with the exception of M when combined with a counteractant (CA) letter produce a chemical reaction in the body called Keltazar. Once a food has been paired with its counteractant, a Keltazarian reaction heats fat cells to piltens which the body then uses for energy. In other words your body becomes a *fat-burning furnace!*

The sometimes unexpected pairing of vowels and consonants disrupts your regular food intake while cleansing your digestive system. It restores and creates a balance in cells, and helps your body absorb enzymes and minerals without even glancing at your digestive system.

The result: A svelte, young, tanned, healthy wrinkle-free body!

Below is the chart with the Please note that there is no effective counterpart for "M" foods so caution is advised. For example you *can't* have 'M'acaroni but you *can* have 'N'oodles, you *can't* have 'M'eat but you *can* have 'B'eef. •*HW*•

Letter	*CA*
A	N
B	O
C	P
D	Q
E	R
F	S
G	T
H	U
I	V
J	W
K	X
L	Y
A	Z

Sample Day:

Breakfast
'E'ggs with a 'R'asher of bacon

Lunch
'G'rilled Cheese with 'T'omato Soup

Dinner
'R'oast Beef with 'E'ggplant

Frequently Asked Questions

Q: My husband is a scientist. Why hasn't he heard of this breakthrough diet?
A: Science is a very personal thing.
Q: You recommend that we walk 4-6 miles a day and restrict our portions to 4 oz or under. Is this the reason that we are losing the weight rather the formula?
A: No.
Q: Gee, it sounds like mumbo-jumbo to me. A diet based on the alphabet—are you sure this isn't a fad diet?
A: The alphabet has been around for thousands of years, we have no reason to believe it's going to run out of steam now.

Tips to make this diet succeed:

• You must make yourself reasonably familiar with the alphabet.

• It is recommended that you walk 4-6 miles per day.

• Keep all portions below 4 oz.

• Drink 12-16 glasses of water every day.

Beauty is its Own Reward

By Jessica Becht

NOT ALL ARE BORN with beauty, but most desire it. Those unpulchritudinous amongst us should remember that there are many types of beauty: beauty of deportment, beauty of dress, or, perhaps most essential, the beauty of self-possession. A woman who is happy, kind, and well mannered will dazzle no matter how awkward her profile.

Yet, a woman who is dissatisfied, jealous, or spiteful will present an unappealing aura despite delicate features.

This sort of old-fashioned advice went out with hats and gloves. Think back to your childhood. How many times did your grandmother admonish you with *Beauty is as beauty does* and other trite aphorisms? She believed in the myth that states *Character counts.* In truth, your grandmother wasn't doing you any favours. She should have stooped down to whisper *Beauty is its own reward* into one of your ears and *It's too bad you were born so homely* into the other.

Thanks to the skewed value system long propagated by the nation's grandmothers, many women have become inept wielders of femininity. Healthy displays of narcissism have been trampled under a propagandist hegemony that values "accomplishment" over mirror gazing. The average woman has forgotten her duty to microscopically scrutinize every feature before leaving her home. Appallingly, many women still do not own such essential beauty enhancing (or, depending on the individual, ugliness minimizing) products as eyebrow shellac, bicuspid bleach, and nipple stain, though benevolent advertisers have long made women aware of the pressing need for such items.

The average woman lacks the courage to consider her features objectively. As her true friends yearn to inform her, her face does not a pretty picture make. However, a true friend never hesitates to interject loving advice such as "Maybe that shade of red just isn't the best for a woman of your sallow complexion," and "Something about your face just doesn't look right to me." Please think of this article as a true and loving friend.

For example, are you one of the many women who have repeatedly failed to select the appropriate shade of mascara? If your lashes are black, a rich mysterious ebony will add even more drama. Yet, some unfortunates have sparse dull lashes of the brown, blonde, or reddish variety. Be honest. Are you one of them? Have you ever considered that the dark mascara that so flatters the genetically gifted has only succeeded in making you look like a phony tramp? Do you really want people to think of you as a broken-down nymphomaniacal bottle-blond in a moth-eaten raccoon coat out trolling for Russian sailors to service? Of course you don't. That's why you should wear brown mascara exclusively.

Lipstick is a universal cosmetic, available to all. But such democratization has only led to abuse. How often are the lips beneath the rose-tinted salve luscious, dare I say noble, enough to merit its benefactions? Be candid. You may be one of the very offenders I speak of. Are your lips thin, perhaps mismatched? Are they creased and shrivelled? And you dare to emphasize such abominations with eye-catching crimson while unemployed plastic surgeons hold signs stating "Will inject silicone microbeads for food." Selfish, selfish woman.

These same surgeons might be employed to sculpt your nose into a less offensive shape. Ask yourself, "Is my nose small, delicately curved, and almost imperceptible?" Have you ever really been consoled by the assertion that your Cyranic profile is "unique"? It is time to realize that uniqueness needn't be an impediment to beauty. Your outsize nose is an opportunity for more beauty, an engraved invitation to the plastic surgeon's office. Sit down with your doctor and be frank. He will be happy to make up an alphabetical list of your flaws. Many doctors offer a multiple procedure discount. Take advantage of it!

Should you be dying your hair? Just between you and me, that brassy shade looks frightful. It's not making you look young, only cheap and striving. I must admit, though, it is preferable to that mouse colour at your roots. Still, blonde is not for everyone. There is good reason why Sophia Loren and Elizabeth Taylor have never bleached their hair. They are infinitely more beautiful as brunettes. Of course, they are also infinitely more beautiful than you.

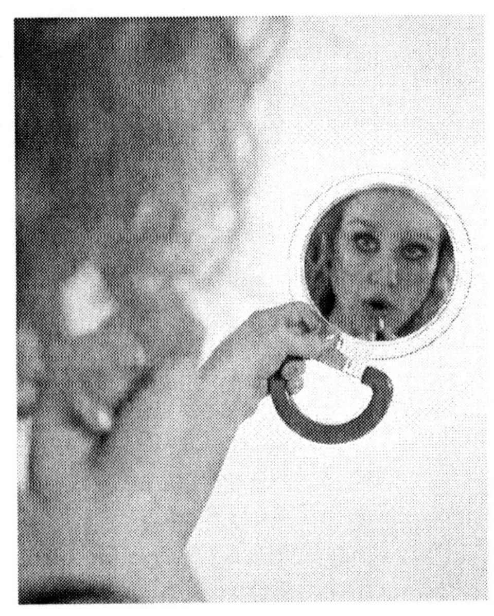

I hope, as this article closes, that a new resolve has been stirring somewhere between your sagging breasts. A good friend (yours truly) has tactfully whispered in your ear. Now you are ready to face your reflection and state, "My ugliness is truly offensive. My obliviousness to this truth has been criminal. I resolve to change and will devote the preponderance of my time, energy, and money to correcting and/ or camouflaging my numerous glaring deformities." Only in this way will you be truly feminine. Remember, beauty is its own reward. •*HW*•

Kidney Theft: How Safe Are You? A Happy Woman Special Report.

By Sharon Grehan

LET'S BE HONEST—when is the last time you gave your kidneys (or for that matter any other internal organ) a second thought?

If you answered "Never," you are not alone. In a recent poll conducted by our janitorial staff we discovered that most citizens of North America, Western Europe and parts of Australia tend to take their kidneys for granted. An astounding 93% percent of us expect our organs to work when needed and when we go out for an evening we expect to wake up with them intact.

However, a brand new kind of thief is changing all that.

Organ harvesters have been targeting men and women all over the world. These thieves dope their unsuspecting victims and then sell their organs, most commonly kidneys, on the black market where a kidney can command up to $10,000.

Kidney theft is one of the leading causes of death in kidney-less people. It is one of the fastest rising crimes in history according to an email we received Tuesday from dave@nospam. Not only does it leave the victim without kidneys it also leaves them feeling ashamed and violated.

A source close to this reporter gave a fourth-hand account of this horrifying crime:

"My friend's cousin's sister Fiona (Editor's note: Fiona is not her real name. Her real name is Mary Kenny) was vacationing in New Orleans. She met a man at a bar and they started talking. They hit it off and he bought her a drink.

The next thing she remembers is waking up in a bathtub filled with ice. There was a phone next to the bathtub with a note taped to it that said 'Call 911.'

Fiona did this and explained the strange circumstances to the 911 operator. The operator, well familiar with organ harvesters, asked Fiona to slowly reach behind and feel if there was a tube protruding out of her back. To her horror, she found one. Luckily the 911 operator had already contacted the ambulance and Fiona was saved."

Fiona was saved, but how safe are you? •*HW*•

How do I know if my kidneys have been stolen? Warning Signs:

- *You may feel the need to urinate more often or less often.*
- *Loss of appetite or experience nausea and vomiting.*
- *Swelling of your hands or feet or numbness.*
- *Drowsiness, trouble concentrating.*
- *Waking up in an unfamiliar hotel room in a bathtub filled with ice with a tube running out of your back and/or an ugly ragged scar below your rib cage.*

Tips to protect your kidneys

- If you are going alone to a bar and a stranger buys you a drink, ask the bartender to take a sip. If the bartender passes out—do not finish the drink.
- If the bartender refuses to test your drink, handcuff yourself to the bar rail. Chances are the thieves will not remove your kidneys in a public place.
- Before you take a sip of the drink mention very casually "I really shouldn't drink as I don't have any kidneys" and cast a sly glance around. If the guy loses interest in you immediately, congratulate yourself on a near-miss.
- Be suspicious of a gent carrying a medical bag if he isn't a doctor.

As with everything an ounce of prevention is worth a pound of cure. You are the most important person you know and your kidneys belong to you and you alone.

Protect yourself.

HW DISPATCH:

Cosmetics Now to be Tested on PETA Members

MAJOR COSMETICS manufacturers, bowing to pressure from the animal rights group People for the Ethical Treatment of Animals, have agreed to suspend all further animal testing and instead will test their products on PETA volunteers.

"We have found that animal testing isn't all that valuable, anyway," said cosmetic scientist Thackery Lavelle. "We only did it to keep the FDA happy. Now that PETA has graciously agreed to get involved, we expect to obtain scientifically valid data on precisely what side effects a woman can expect if she inadvertently dumps 12 grams of eyeshadow into her eye during the course of her morning beautification ritual."

Not everyone at PETA supports the measure, however. A splinter faction of the group's membership picketed the press conference, apparently objecting to the names of proposed lip and nail colour lines for fall. "We won't stand for Tantalizing Tangerine," shouted one bearded protester. "It's patently offensive to citrus fruits, which may or may not be as enticing, alluring or provocative as this name implies." No word yet on how the cosmetics companies will handle this new boycott threat. —*E. Hanes*

Woman has Half a Notion not to Tip Hairdresser

At a press conference on her front lawn, attended by three neighborhood children, two dogs, and a mildly curious passerby, Olivia Wingfield of Medicine Hat, Alberta, announced that she nearly decided not to tip her hairdresser Monday. "I wasn't entirely pleased with the cut," Wingfield stated, "and I had half a notion not to leave a tip. It wasn't a fully formed notion, however, so I decided not to go with it." Wingfield reports she wound up leaving a $2 tip on a $20 cut. The hairdresser in question was not identified and had no comment. —*E. Hanes*

•*HW*•

"...as I told the Newark police, I really have no idea how she fell down that stairwell..."

The Rules of Family: Advice from Donna Corleone

By Pamela Monk

DEAR MADRONE,

Ten years ago, when I was down in the dumps, my mother, may she rest in peace, wasn't doing so hot, and my son was running around with a no good tramp, may she rest in peace as well, and as I told the Newark police, I really have no idea how she fell down that stairwell, and my arthritis was really bad, until I went on this diet, no nightshades, it works, no tomatoes, no eggplant, no potatoes, I swear by it now, but this was before it started working, I was complaining to my good friend Lorraine, and she gave me a list of principles to live by that she had cut out from your column. Well you know how things go, I had it on my refrigerator, but it broke down and when the people from Home Depot delivered the new one, I wasn't there, my other son, who is good, but dim, let them take away the old one without removing any of the magnets and the things they were holding on. Could you run it again for me? I want to give it to my cousin's daughter-in-law who doesn't seem to know her elbow from her you know what, excuse my French.

Thanks, Connie from Bayonne.

Dear Connie,
I am very happy to oblige you. Every few years, it doesn't hurt to remind people of how things actually are, as opposed to the way people wish things would be.
God Bless, Donna.

1.Never get in between someone and their mother. If you just followed only this rule you'd be better off than 90% of the *mamalukes* out there who have no sense.
2. Never refuse family a favour.
3. Never ask family for something you know they can't give.
4. Never believe it's just about the money.
5. Never pretend it's nice when it's not.
6. Never expect thanks when you kick someone in the teeth.
7. Never mix up the people who have what you want with the people who want what you have.
8. Never fight a battle you know you can't win, except if your honour is involved, then always fight it.

There is more, but these are the main ones.
God Bless, Donna
•*HW*•

"Every few years, it doesn't hurt to remind people of how things actually are..."

Chapter Two – February

His Secret Thoughts!

By Sharon Grehan

WHAT IS HE REALLY thinking when you're at a wedding or spooning peacefully *après amour*? For years science and television have told us that whenever he has an idle moment his thoughts are of you, his beloved. But is that true?

For the first time ever in the history of the world we asked men to tell us what they are really thinking and actually listened to the answers! Yay for us!

The men who participated in the study were all coincidentally named John Doe so we changed the names in the interests of variety.

Joseph

Whenever I go to a wedding I always find myself wondering how hot the groom must be in his tux. I wonder why the minister always needs to hold a book because you'd think he'd have it memorized by now unless he's new. I wonder how they train a new minister. Do they have an old minister stand by to correct you if you say something stupid like maybe mix up Judas for Jesus?

I sometimes wonder how much it would cost to heat a church and whether or not I could stand living with such high ceilings. I try to figure out how much paint you'd need to do the ceiling and wonder if you'd have to build a scaffold or if you could rent one. If you built one then you'd have it again if you ever needed to repaint but where would you keep it?

I then figure out if you had a church you'd probably have room for a pretty big garage so there would be lots of room for stuff like scaffolding and you could put plywood across the scaffold and use it for shelves when you aren't using it for painting.

I could probably get a motorcycle and put spare parts on the scaffold. I'd put it at one end and I'd have a workbench at the other end. I'd get a fridge, a comfy chair and a radio and put them in the middle.

I sometimes wonder what the bridesmaid looks like naked but it depends on the wedding.

Michael

After we make love and my wife is snuggled up next to me, she usually asks me what I'm thinking. I used to say nothing but I realized that's the wrong answer so I tell her I'm thinking about her. What I'm usually thinking about though, is a ham sandwich.

Not the packaged kind of ham but the good meaty kind of ham, the kind you get at Christmas. I picture a huge Kaiser roll smothered in hot mustard with a very small layer of butter, sometimes I put lettuce on it but not always, I plop on a nice big slice of Swiss and finish it off with a slice of beefsteak tomato.

I imagine myself washing this down with a nice cold beer while sitting on the porch watching the guys across the street doing construction. I think of how cool it would be to be paid to smash things with a hammer. I wonder if you get really good at it if they give you a nickname like 'Demolition Man.' I try to remember if there was a Demolition Man superhero and then I wonder what happened to my old comic books and if they'd be worth something today. Then I wonder what kind of sandwiches the construction guys have then I start thinking of the ham sandwich again.

Gregory

When we go furniture shopping, I think of the couch I would design if I had the time. It would be big and soft, long enough to stretch out on without my feet hanging over the edge. It would have a beverage holder and a remote built into the arm. If I put it on wheels I could rig up some kind of pulley so that I could wheel my way over to the bathroom or the kitchen.

I'd have a phone installed and the fabric would be soft but coated with a material that would make stains slip off it. Like silicone or Teflon. I wonder if I had a Teflon suit if I would keep slipping off seats or do they have a bit of a tread.

When the salesman starts talking I usually wonder how much a job like that pays and how much commission he is getting. While she's talking to him about material and sage green I wonder what ever happened to corduroy and what is a sage. I find myself thinking about Kung Fu and wondering if I could take David Carradine in a fight now that he's an alcoholic. I think of how cool it would be just travelling from town to town and then I wonder whatever happened to hobos who used to ride the rails. I think about how I'd get a dog if I was a hobo.

They start talking about flame retardants and I wonder how long it would take the place to burn up if there was ever a fire and how if I was a firefighter I'd make sure I was the driver so that I could honk and wave to kids but be the last one that actually makes it into the fire. Then I wonder about how much insurance they must pay until my wife tells me which couch is perfect for us.

Gary

Whenever my wife and I have "a talk" my first reaction is to run through the week and find out what I did wrong.

When I have it narrowed down to three she usually finds something that I didn't even think of. While she tells me about how I embarrassed, humiliated or hurt her I try to figure out ways of fixing it.

When she rejects all my suggestions I try figure out how she expects to sort things out when she won't let me fix anything so I end up just staring a lot and wondering how big a thing this is on a scale of one to ten.

I notice that when she is in earnest her head goes up and down a lot like the dog we used to have in our '72 Chevy. I wonder what happened to that dog and try to remember if it had eyes that worked like brake lights or if they were just glass. Then

I try to remember if we got the Country Squire right after the Chevy and then I wonder why they put fake wood panelling on it. I think of all the seating the Country Squire had with the fold down jump seat in the back and I wonder if anyone ever got squished to death in it. I think about how your hair and your nails are supposed to grow after you're dead and I think about what it's like to be dead and imagine that I have a Skeletor robot head and then my wife tells me to stop making weird faces and I'm back to not helping with our relationship.

• • •

Well there you have it! Isn't it just typical that every single man answered incorrectly! If you are like the HW staff you may find the results startling and a little boring. You might want to do what we did and ignore them.

Vive la difference! •*HW*•

The Happy Woman Soup Diet

By Sharon Grehan

THIS DIET IS GUARANTEED to melt off the pounds and make you happier and more desirable than you have ever been! While other diets rely on tiresome choices and confusing food groups, this diet is a breeze – the simplest diet for the simplest Happy Woman!

Day One	
breakfast	soup
lunch	soup
dinner	soup
snack	soup
Day Two	
breakfast	soup
lunch	soup
dinner	soup
snack	soup
Day Three	
breakfast	soup
lunch	soup
dinner	soup
snack	soup

Repeat the rotation. (See handy clip & save chart.) For added variety you may change the days around. For example: Day Two, Day One, Day Three or Day Three, Day Two, Day One but please try to avoid a rotation of Day Three, Day One and Day Two.

Notes of caution:

You may find your thought processes slow as the brain burns ketones, so put off any major decisions until you are thin.

Ketone bodies can accumulate in the blood and cause dehydration, nausea, weakness, dizziness and ketones are sometimes produced by the liver at levels high enough to be toxic to the brain.

It is best not to exercise on this diet as this may lead to Metabolic Acidosis (buildup of ketones toxic to brain function).This could lead to coma and ultimately death.

You may experience toxic accumulations in the colon and the loss of teeth and hair. If this happens it is recommended that you add a whole wheat cracker.

Once you come off the diet you may find that you regain all the weight within 48 hours. To avoid this we recommend staying on the diet. •*HW*•

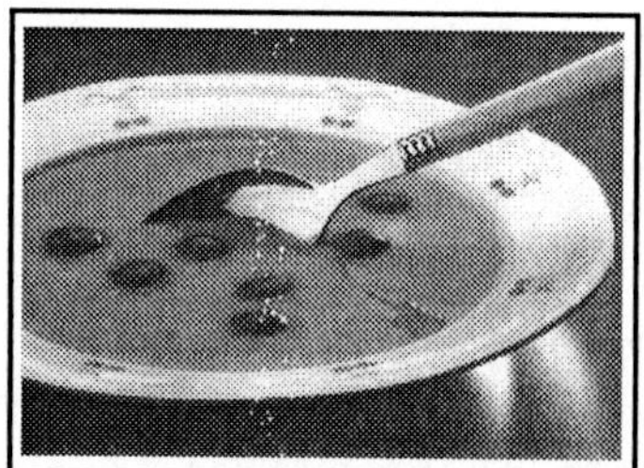

Clip & Save

Handy Rotation Reminder

If you start the diet on a Saturday:

Saturday - Day One
Sunday - Day Two
Monday - Day Three
Tuesday - Day One
Wednesday - Day Two
Thursday - Day Three
Friday - Day One
Saturday - Day Two

If you start the diet on a Saturday: use the above and replace Saturday with Sunday, Sunday with Monday, Monday with Tuesday, Tuesday, with Wednesday, Wednesday with Thursday, Thursday with Friday, Friday with Saturday.

If you start the diet on a Sunday: replace Monday with Tuesday, Tuesday with Wednesday, Wednesday with Thursday, Thursday with Friday, Friday with Saturday, Saturday with Sunday.

Don't start the diet on a Tuesday.

Libby Interviews the Man Who Analyzes James Gandolfini's Trash

By Sharon Grehan

WE TELEPHONED Mr. Gandolfini (Tony Soprano from *The Sopranos*) and his people several times and they wouldn't return our calls. What is it with celebs these days? In the old days stars were trotted out like show ponies. They answered questions, they got their pictures taken and they loved it whether they liked it or not.

So instead, we are happy to have a borough-renowned Trash Analyst, Norton Jameson. He has been studying Mr. Gandolfini for over three years now and hopefully he will give us some insight into the man who is too much of a big shot to talk to a lowly journalist.

Libby: I'd love to ask you some questions about how you got started in this field but my readers don't care about you so let's get to Mr. Gandolfini.
Norton: I've been studying Mr. Gandolfini's trash every Thursday for three years now and what can I tell you? The man is fascinating – once you see the photographs and the results I'm sure you'll agree. He is a mass of contradictions.

For example, in this photo you see a juice box, four Snackin' Grahams, one Dove Bar, three tablespoons of rice, two corn husks an empty tin of Classic Gold Bond Triple Action Powder...
Libby: That's a very nice picture frame. Is it gilt?
Norton: Thank you, yes it is. This particular grouping reveals to me that this is the trash of a risk-taker.
Libby: That's fascinating! How are you able to tell this from mounds of garbage?
Norton: Well the garbage can, like the human head, is filled with things. The difficulty is knowing how to read these things, being able to translate or interpret them. Luckily, over time I've developed a highly scientific system and it has an accuracy rate of 99.8%.

By measuring Rapid Influx with Staid Driving and using Justifiable Endorsement as my Median Risk Assessor, I'm able to paint a very accurate picture of any human being.

Here is another example from the Gandolfini file:

Chili seeds, an orange peel and deep-fried mozzarella remnants reveal a very complex man who likes jazz but hates jazz musicians. Also with this particular combination I feel unless he is very careful Mr. Gandolfini could be at risk. I would suggest he stay away from elevators and beach umbrellas until the end of October to the beginning of early November.

In this one, the dental floss, coffee grounds, paper cup and Nutrigrain bar wrapper, reveal Mr. Gandolfini's ability to improvise rhyming couplets while the Breath Assure, the advertising flyer for aluminum siding, the store brand toilet paper and quarter spool of thread display his fascination with steam engines. The second grouping also reveals some conflict with a male authority figure. Could be his father, an uncle perhaps a priest, police officer or the pope? A few tablespoons of coffee grounds and some turnip rind would probably balance this out.

These shopping bags are very interesting. Notice that they are neatly folded and placed one inside of the other. One would think the subject was hoarding or saving the bags for another purpose, but as you can see the first bag (the primary bag) is full of used bags. Instead of reusing the bags as one would anticipate, Mr. Gandolfini simply threw all of them out. This I feel illustrates his willingness to learn foreign languages.

There is an element of impulsiveness in Mr. Gandolfini's makeup. The butter wrapper, the heel of bread, the newspaper, clearly show this, but the empty jam jar, the receipt for the Leo Sayer CD, the apple core and the sock with the hole in it reveal that though Mr. Gandolfini may have impulsive tendencies, he tends to curb them a great deal of the time. The one that concerned me most was the evidence presented here: A cereal box, three eggshells, one half can of beans, a milk carton and four toast crusts; these all point to an obsessive-compulsive disorder.

"There is an element of impulsiveness in Mr. Gandolfini's makeup."

Libby: I just had a thought–are you sure all this garbage is his?
Norton: Yes, of course.
Libby: But how can you be so sure?
Norton: Well, the toss factor, a forensic method similar to blood patterning, gives every indication that Mr. Gandolfini was the sole thrower. Also, no one else in his house is famous so I why would I analyze their trash? That would be stupid.
Libby: Well this has been simply fascinating I thank you perhaps you could come back again some time! Who do you plan on analyzing next?
Norton: It all depends on the route the city gives me.
Libby: It's been a pleasure.
•*HW*•

Your Career in Sales

By Elaine Langlois

IF YOU ARE FRESH out of high school, or have gone to college and somehow failed to get your M.R.S., or are seeking a change in lifestyle, you will find that there is practically nothing as satisfying, outside of marrying a billionaire, as a career in sales.

Qualities and skills.

What qualities and skills do you need for a career in sales? Not any! You do not need people skills or a work ethic or a sense of responsibility or common sense or even basic math, since the cash register does it for you. Oh, you may need a little math to figure out your employee discount, if you bother to buy things instead of simply taking them home.

Your Career Path

With a career in sales, you can rise rapidly up the escalator of success: Shopper/Shoplifter → Sales Associate → Associate Manager → Managerial Associate → Managerial Manager → Sergeant Major → Major Major → Yossarian → Branch Manager from Kansas City → Head of Macy's Parade → Martha Stewart.

But we do not want to give you the impression that working in sales is easy. It is not all trying on designer clothes and lipstick, getting first dibs on merchandise, and being supercilious to customers. Distasteful as it may sound, working in sales can sometimes involve actual work.

Telephone etiquette.

A ringing phone can usually be ignored, or you can frisk through a series of buttons to route the call to Automotive Supplies. Occasionally, however, say after the 23rd ring, you just might have to answer.

Telephone etiquette is very important. When you answer the phone, you give the customer her first impression of the company. Be sure it is the right one!

1. Speak as rapidly as possible: *Thankyouforcallingblockb ustervideocanihelpyou.*

Strive for a droning tone. You should sound bored, put-upon, and even a little whiny.

2. Let the customer ask her question. Then reply indifferently: *Letmecheckforyoupleasehold.*

3. Put her on hold and leave her there until she hangs up. Or get a computer to reply, or better yet, two.

Helping customers.

It is really too tedious for you to have to work for a living, let alone deal with customers. Happily, a career in sales requires little contact with the public. In fact, the number of employees actually "helping" customers decreases proportionally to the number of customers, according to the well-known mathematical formula:

Let x = the number of sales associates on the floor and let y = the number of customers

$$\int \frac{dx}{\cosh^3 ax} - \frac{\tanh ax}{2a \cosh ax} + \frac{1}{2a} \tan^{-1} \sinh ax$$

If Johnny can bake 36 dozen cookies in 5 days, how far will he have to ride his bike to get to school?

As the line at the single open checkout lane lengthens, cluster in small groups with other employees, talking and laughing, or amble idly about. Make sure the customers can see you.

Retailers are gradually shaping the expectations of customers so they will be used not only to having no help whatsoever but to actually serving themselves. Witness the rise of automated checkout lines in grocery stores. Here, in a sadistic sort of role reversal, you can sit behind a desk and read *Teen Vogue* while customers scan their own groceries and bag them, shepherded through the process by rude, dull, unintuitive machines.

If a customer approaches you, don't panic. Grab the nearest phone and start talking. Take out one of those UPC-checker gizmos and wave it at merchandise. If the customer manages to ask you something, tell her pleasantly that you will find out for her. Then walk away and don't come back.

Indifferent Service.

The concept of Indifferent Service is fast gaining hold in sales establishments across the continent. Here are a few guidelines for restaurants:

1. Show customers to the table, and before they have actually seated themselves, ask for their drink orders.

2. If they "need a minute," disappear for twenty.

3. Bring them tea without cream or spoons, Coke without fizz, scotch in a dirty glass, etc.

4. Ignore glares and hand signals, and secretly laugh at customers stirring black tea with forks.

5. Make diners wait 45 minutes for their food and then rush them through the meal to make room for the next set of customers. There are many ways to do this. One is to whip away each plate once they are down to the last few mouthfuls.

Diners are unlikely to protest because they won't want to seem piggy. If they still linger, slap down the bill (with 15 percent gratuity included), and bring in the next group of customers—preferably with small, ill-behaved children—to hover around their table.

Handling complaints.

It is inevitable that customers will complain about a product. When this happens, don't argue. The correct response is to blame the customer's dissatisfaction on the customer. Example:

This bra doesn't fit me right.

Your answer:

You're probably bigger on one side than the other.

There you have it: the beginnings of what is likely to be a very pleasurable climb to success. Put yourself before the customer, the company before the customer, and yourself before the company, and you are on your way to the top in a career in sales! •*HW*•

"The correct response is to blame the customer's dissatisfaction on the customer..."

No Sew Do-It-Yourself Peasant Blouse

By Crystal Click

AS IF YOU DIDN'T know, this year's must have item is the Peasant Blouse. The ultimate in retro-wear, you (or your mother) will no doubt remember its most recent flirt with popularity in the early 80s, the 60s, the 40s and every 20 years prior dating back to the serfs of Medieval France. This proves once and for all the inherit value of Feudalism, even the impoverished were smartly dressed.

Speaking of poverty, if your bank book looks to have been ravaged by marauding warmongers you can still stay in favour with the fashion lords. With a little ingenuity and a lot of tape you can have your own peasant blouse for $1.99 or less.

To create your shirt, you will need:

- Two kitchen size garbage bags, white preferably
- Double sided carpet tape.
- Transparent Tape
- Clear packing tape.
- A hole punch.
- A shoe lace.
- Permanent marker
- Scissors

There is very little measuring in this project. The optimum peasant blouse is white and billowy. A properly fitting peasant blouse glides over your curves effortlessly causing casual onlookers and observant neighbors to murmur, "is she pregnant, or is it that tent she's wearing?" Additionally, the snow white colour will give you that pasty washed out look so sought after by the penniless and ill-fed. •*HW*•

Step 1. If you are an earth friendly DIYer and prefer to use recycled trash bags, thoroughly rinse away any coffee grounds or stray particles from last week's lasagna. The mood is provincial, not white trash.

Cut straight across the sealed end on both bags.

Step 2. Fold both bags in half lengthwise. About six inches down, draw a line on each bag at a 45 degree angle. Cut on the line.

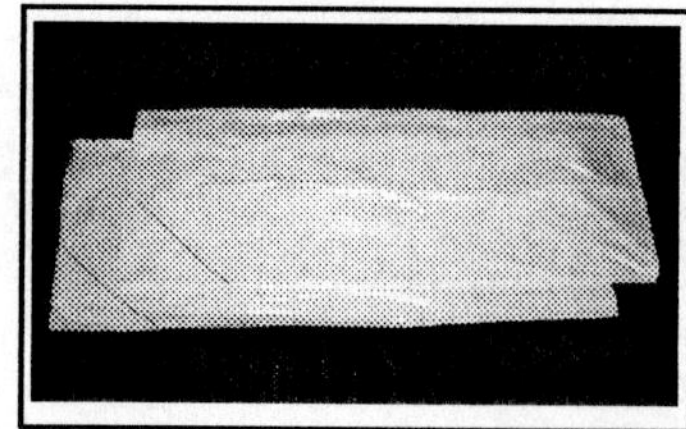

Step 3. Take one bag and cut lengthwise on each side. You should have two pieces identical to the picture below. These are the sleeves. Do not cut the remaining bag open, it forms the body of the garment.

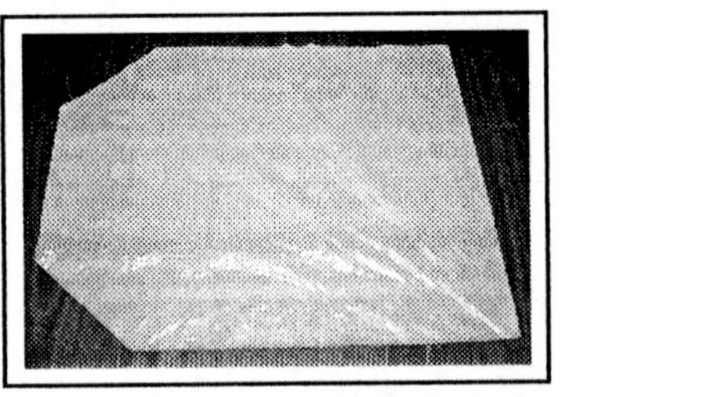

Step 4. Lay out one sleeve piece on your work table, diagonal corners together. Cut a piece of double sided carpet tape the length of the sleeve. Unless the tape is very narrow, you will want to cut it in half lengthwise to avoid bulk at the seams. Apply tape to one long edge of the arm piece. Lap the other long edge over the first, forming a long tube. Repeat steps 1 through 4 because, at this point, it is 99% likely that you have taped your finger or your instructions to the garbage bag. Stretched and torn plastic is unsightly. Repeat Step 4 again, as most people prefer two sleeves.

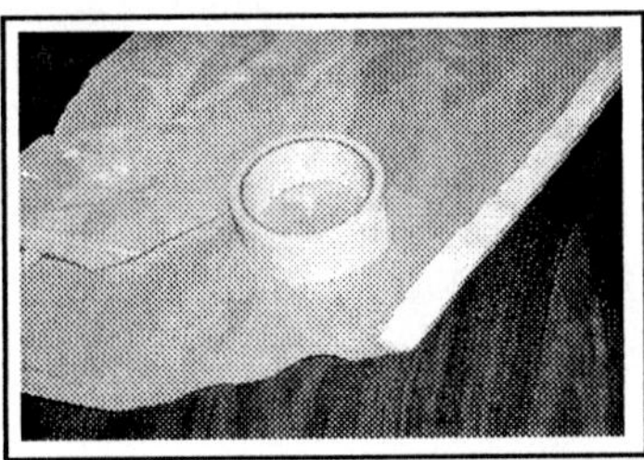

Step 5. Cut one piece of double sided carpet tape the length of one side of the "V" formed by the sleeve. Cut the tape into four pieces lengthwise. Match the "V" on each side of the bodice with the "V" on the upper end of each arm tube and tape in place.

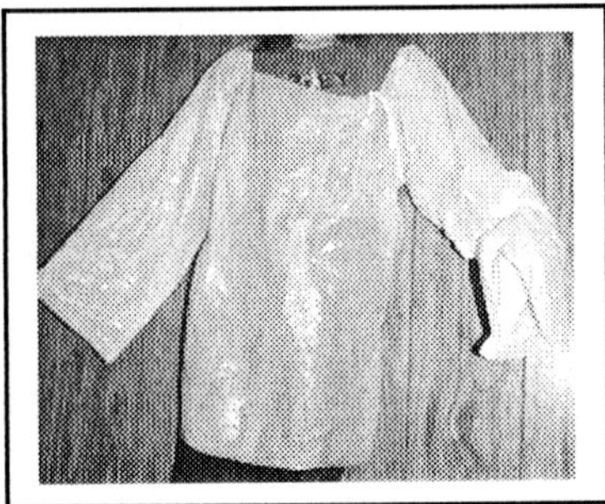

Step 6. Next, gather the neckline and sleeves, securing with transparent tape.

Step 7. Form the front placket with a vertical six inch strip of packing tape. Place an additional strip on the inside for durability. Notch the placket to whatever depth you are comfortable with.

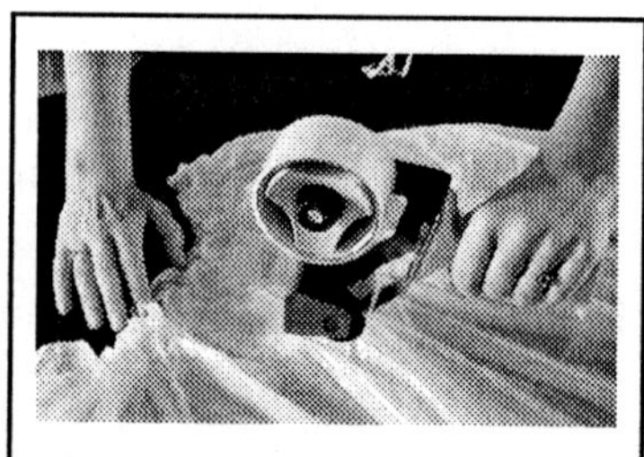

Step 8. With a hole punch, fashion six symmetrical holes for the lacing.

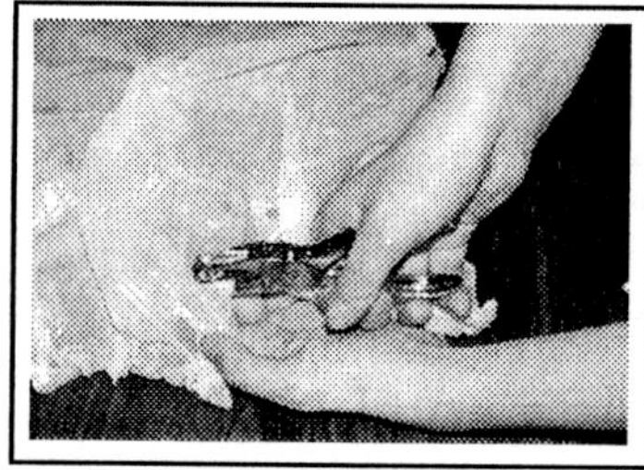

Step 9. Lace up the front and wear for crop tilling and other social activities.
Easy to care for, just hose off and drip-dry!
Caution: Avoid open flames while constructing and/or wearing your garment.

photos by C. Click

Herstory: Jane Smith–Leaving the House

By Meredith Litt

AN ORIGINAL FILM brought to you by The Domestication Network: Television to Scare Ambitious Women into Spinsterhood

In perhaps its most chilling production yet, The Domestication Network has unveiled a controversial new film starring Virginia McMaiden as the ambitious Jane Smith.

Jane Smith is a 30 year-old woman still living under her parents' roof. Because they have provided for her since infancy, she has not left the house since graduating from high school, reassured by her parents that there is nothing of value beyond their white picket fence. However, after spending an evening at home with her high school friends (who are all college alumnae), she decides that she wants to step outside the confines of her childhood home and experience adulthood.

What follows is a terrifying portrait of the risk a woman takes when she attempts to assert her independence. As Jane's hand reaches for the brass doorknob, we feel her sense of terror as the wind, the demonic respiration of the "outside" world, pushes the hair from her face. Within minutes, she is exposed to pathogens, carcinogens, evil men (one whom she marries that very night on a whim, and another who stalks her), and identity thieves lurking in the background every time she enters a store to purchase business attire.

These threats are only the prologue to a week-long story that includes an amoral stalker, an identity thief obsessed with her perfect body, a mugging, a virulent case of strep throat from a germ-ridden doorknob, negative self-esteem, pubic lice from a public toilet seat, and a husband whose abuse is so relentless that I found myself holding my breath until the film's shocking ending, during which Jane meets with policy makers to eradicate the entire women's lib movement and offers a compelling, heart-wrenching speech about how freedom has destroyed her life. When she finally returns to her parents' house in the last scene, a voice-over reassures us that Jane Smith went on to spend the rest of her life crocheting and making quilts. The viewing audience breathes a collective sigh of relief at the good news after being taken for a 90-minute roller coaster ride.

Before viewing this film, I never realized just how inherently perilous it is for women to venture outside the domestic realm. Thank God for these riveting films on Domestication, which are played in rapid enough succession to keep a woman glued to her couch for entire weekends.

We, as women, owe our lives and sense of safety to this network for protecting us from the countless predators in this cruel, vicious world. Kudos to a medium brave enough to explore the dastardly consequences of female independence and suffrage. Kudos to a medium strong enough to compel women everywhere to shun financial independence in favour of one more affirming story from a network acclaimed by some of today's most backward-thinking talk show hosts.

Next time any of you women viewers think of trying to get a job or college degree, watch *Leaving the House*, only on Domestication. If you are smart, you'll think again. •*HW*•

"Did they have a secret? Indeed they did..."

Giddy Over Girdles

By Jessica Becht

THE MALLOMAR AND cigarette diet has forsaken you, just like all the others, leaving you as paunchy, cellulite-pocked, and bloated as at the launch of your latest regime. You seethe bitterly. The women of your grandmother's generation maintained lithe figures despite gorging on butter pats, hollandaise sauce, and quivering coconut cream pies set in tender lard crusts. Did they have a secret? Indeed they did. It was called a "girdle."

Perhaps the name of this special item rings familiar? It's time to yank one on, tubby. Yes, you. However, before investing in the industrial-strength corsetry you will surely require, you may want to study up on constricting undergarments. You will likely need an assortment of girdles to address varied figure flaws, from thunder thighs to a waistline of dimensions more usual to livestock.

You must first analyze your form before a full length three-way mirror. Sway to the soothing hum of fluorescent lighting as you ponder your defects. Friends and family members will enjoy taking helpful notes. Do love handles, a protuberant gut, swollen behind, or corpulent thighs mar your sylphlike potential? Perhaps all of the above? Let a light-hearted debate determine which of your figure flaws is most repellent. Resolve to disguise your failings with the proper undergarment.

For the woman with billows of stomach

fat, a waist cincher is a smart choice. Rigid corsetry can reduce a waistline by up to four inches. There is one caveat, however. That excess of adipose must go somewhere, and is apt to find your hips most obliging. You can disguise these unusual proportions with clever fashion choices. A fitted dirndl skirt is a first-rate option. Though you may long to flaunt your new waistline in a sassy cropped tee, remember that an exposed girdle will spoil the illusion. Geriatric foundation garments lack the playful sex appeal of thong and bra straps.

If an epic rear end is your primary blemish, select a girdle that will shift some of that lumpish flesh to your abdomen. You may then highlight your newly android hips in an über-fitted pencil skirt. Because significant displacement will occur, a loose tunic is a must. Elude all embraces while clad in this costume, lest the burgeoning contours of your waistline place you under suspicion of having shoplifted several packages of jumbo marshmallows.

Those of colossal thigh girth will hail a long-line undergarment with the vigor to compress their cellulite-riddled limbs, allowing a lissome silhouette in spandex pants. Yet, how to obfuscate the inevitable above-the-knee bulges? You might take advantage of a retro fashion trend and conceal these bizarre protuberances with chunky legwarmers.

Strive not to show the strain in your face while trussed in the asphyxiating undergarment that is right for you. Aim for a relaxed expression and an easygoing, if breathless, simper.

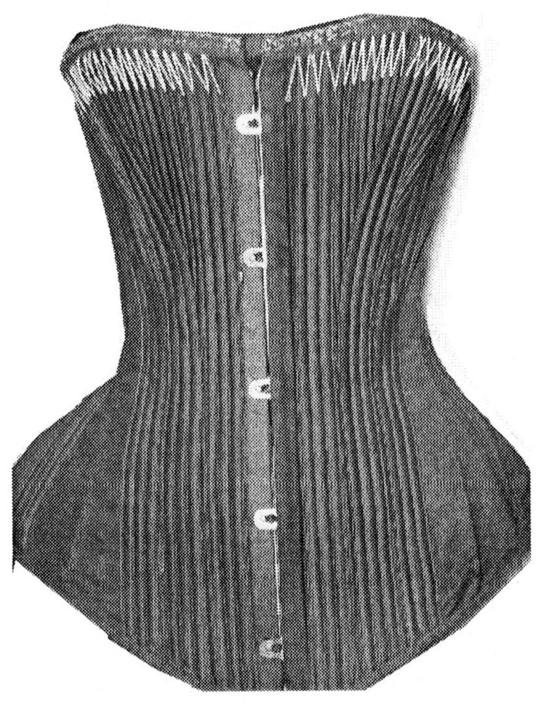

Acquaintances will surely pry about the willowy new outlines of your once sinewless figure, pumping you for diet tips amidst sly inquiries about wasting diseases. Never admit to needing reinforcements. Instead, concoct some malicious nonsense about skunk cabbage and vitamin loaf. In fact, watching your friends try to down these delicacies might help you smirk your way to a trimmer figure. •*HW*•

HW DISPATCH:

Clown College Grad Accused of Plagiarism

Scuttlebutt, (Ernest Mundson) a recent graduate of Chuckles Academy has been asked to turn in his nose by school officials.

Reviewing the final exams, officials discovered that Mundson's essay "The Art of Spritz" was actually written in 1942 by Googlio (Enrico Rosarez).

This is not the first time Mundson, famous in Skylark for falling down while running and pulling a seemingly never-ending hanky from his pocket, has been in the hotseat.

Dryden area clown Klosso called Scuttlebutt a "big fat booger" and sued him for stealing his "frightened-by-little-dog-scale-a-telephone-pole" routine. The case was settled out of court for an undisclosed sum and an apology, but Scuttlebutt was in the news again last month when Stinky MacElwaine accused him of lifting his famous "sad-face-happy-face."

Mundson, interviewed at his trailer in Skylark issued a denial. "If you want to find similarities in anything you will, if you look hard enough. For example apples and oranges. Apples are round, oranges are round, apples have seeds, oranges have seeds—do you see where I'm going with this?" Mundsen then attempted to juggle the fruit and after five attempts gave up, pulled down his pants and squirted this reporter with a chrysanthemum.
—*S. Grehan*

Couple Cancels Marriage due to Low Ratings

Emily and Paul Bainbridge, the lead actors in the Morton-Bainbridge union, jointly announced the marriage has been pulled from the fall schedule. "After seven successful years, we've had to face the reality of declining interest in our daily show," Paul Bainbridge said. "Frankly, we felt we'd exhausted all possible storylines, leaving these characters with no room for growth," Emily Bainbridge said. Paul admitted that the creative relationship had sometimes been rocky, but denied reports that salary inequities were to blame for the cancellation. "I've never begrudged Emily her larger salary, even though I felt we both contributed equally to the success of the series," he said, to which Emily replied, "Now it comes out. He's always been jealous of my salary and has resented my surging career." Emily, who has already lined up a guest appearance with Brad Winthrop on his evolving psychodrama *A Series of Affairs*, plans to take a brief vacation after her contract expires. Fans of the Morton-Bainbridge show planned to hold parties marking the series finale, to be performed live in the courtroom of District Judge William Goldblum, and watch re-runs of the couple's home movies. "Tuesday night fondue just isn't going to be the same without Emily and Paul," sniffed long-time fan Mary Hollingsworth. —*E. Hanes*

The Rules of Family: Advice from Donna Corleone

By Pamela Monk

DEAR MADRONE,

Please help me decide what I should do. My sister Rosa is married to a guy, who shall we say, makes a gorilla look *piccolo.* He has a good heart, not malicious. He is strong, who doesn't like a strong man, that's how it should be.

Unfortunately, last month, at a family barbecue, he decides to demonstrate his muscle by grabbing my brother Frankie's wife around the neck and nearly choking her to death. Frankie's wife was more than a little put out, I can't say I blame her, I thought her eyes were going to pop out of her head if she didn't suffocate first. Rosa says he meant no harm, Frankie's wife should get over herself. So here's the problem. Frankie's wife pressed charges against Rosa's husband, and I am in the middle. Who should I side with?

I am,
Torn, Park Slope

Dear Torn,

Eh, *comsi comsa*, you know what I'm saying? You could say it's between your brother-in-law and your sister-in-law, neither of them directly family, so let them kill each other, unless of course it was at your house, and you may have rules about that, in which case you have a beef with them both. However, each of them is married to a relative of yours with equal claims on your allegiance. How to decide?

Power, of any kind, can of course be wielded for its own sake, that's why it's power. But just because you *can* do something doesn't mean you *should.* For a family to run smoothly power must be used only in the interests of justice and safety. If the throttling was whimsical, as you describe, then you must side with Frankie and his wife.

Whatever you do, though, someone will be angry with you, double if you do nothing. That's how that goes. What were they eating? You might want to avoid that next time you barbecue.

God bless, Donna

•*HW*•

Chapter Three – March

Fast Food Weight Loss Challenge

By Sharon Grehan

INSPIRED BY THAT big-mawed Subway hawker Jared, Celia Pratt (our fashion editor) thought it would be a hoot to dip a toe in the Health and Fitness pool and try a fast food experiment on her own. Our Health and Fitness editor Joan Dryden interviewed Celia Pratt in the very stylish HW office.

Joan: Celia tell me about your little experiment.

Celia: Well Joan, first off before we go any further, do you mind removing that neck scarf? Your neck is so short it looks like your head is ready for harvesting.

Anyway, we took three fa... uh, "generously proportioned" (Gawd a person can't even open their mouth these days!) ladies and had them pick their fave fast food franchise. We did a weigh-in and then had them eat nothing but their fast food for a whole month.

Joan: How did you monitor their progress? Did you have a nurse or a doctor keep tabs?

Celia: No, they're interns so we just sent them home with a tablet of paper and a couple of 2Bs. We told them to keep a diary and come back in a month. But...drumroll please (Gawd that's funny because this is going to be written down isn't it? And how do you spell drrrrrrrrrr) here are their diet diary excerpts and the results!

Subject: Jane

Restaurant: Taco Bell

I was really looking forward to this. I've always loved Taco Bell and this seemed easy to follow. I stuck to their plain taco. Following Jared's example (he ate only one type of sub) I thought I'd do the same and stick to the to the plain taco.

Diary Excerpts

Week One: So far so good! I found the tacos filling and satisfying. I had one for breakfast, one for lunch, one for dinner and one as a snack! A part of me feels like a naughty schoolgirl for being able to eat all this goodness!

Week Two: The lack of variety was getting to me so I decided to change things around by leaving lettuce out of one and tomatoes out of another. The customer service reps won't do this for you, you have to do it yourself. Even though I come in three times a day and ask for exactly the same thing they never get the order right. So God forbid they should help me.

Week Three: I drank four packets of hot sauce just to see if my tongue still works.

Week Four: The song *Fascinatin' Rhythm* keeps going through my head and I've been throwing up since last Friday. I can't hold anything down I feel like I'm going to die. If I hadn't received my Visa bill I would be absolutely certain that I'm already dead and in

hell.
Start Weight: 138
End Weight: 130
Total Loss: 8 Lbs

Subject: Rachel
Restaurant: Pizza Hut
Love the 'za! I remember in college I practically lived on pizza, this is going to be great!
Diary Excerpts
Week One: Not bad at all. I've got a bit of heartburn and it's a little boring but no big whoop.
Week Two: I've tried every pizza they make and you know what? Every meal kind of tastes like dough with sauce and cheese. I really, really miss salad. And eggs. Boiled eggs, fried eggs, egg salad. Oh and fruit. I'd sell my sister's kidneys for an orange.
Week Three: I got up late this morning and I don't care. What's the point? I missed breakfast, I'm going to miss lunch on purpose and I don't care if I die before dinner. I just don't really care.
Week Four: My teeth are loose.
Start Weight: 121
End Weight: 114
Total Loss: 7 Lbs

Subject: Michaela
Restaurant: KFC
My choice was KFC. Ever since I was a kid I've loved this finger licking goodness. Although the menu is rather limited I just know that I will never, ever, ever get sick of the Colonel.
Diary Excerpts
Week One: Had a chicken sandwich for breakfast (Hold the mayo!) crispy wings for lunch and a three piece for dinner. Have I died and gone to heaven? Even my skin looks better! Everyone I've met has remarked upon my glow! My energy isn't great, but it hasn't been since the reality TV craze started.
Week Two: The glow was actually chicken grease. Weird huh? Ha ha ha ha ha ha ha ha ha. You wouldn't think grease would actually seep through your pores. Ha ha ha ha ha ha ha. I ate four days ago or today. Hahahahahaha.
Week Three: I had a dream a clown riding scissors was chasing me. He kept exposing himself and laughing maniacally—I tried to outrun him but he pinned me down and spat orange rind into my face. I woke up in a cold sweat and I still feel frightened.
Week Four: I haven't had a bowel movement in two weeks. I can't feel my feet and I punched a parking lot attendant. I hate you and the whole staff of HW. If I ever get better I will sue you and punish you for what you have done to me. I hate you I hate you I hate you.
Start Weight: 144
End Weight: 130
Total Loss: 14 Lbs

Celia: Da da da dah! The winner is KFC!
Joan: From the diaries Michaela is just short of delirious, she hasn't had a bowel movement in weeks and can't feel her feet.

Celia: And she lost 14 pounds! KFC is clearly the best fast food diet choice.
Joan: Yes, but all of the women seemed to have lost the weight because they stopped eating.
Celia: Absolutely, and there is a lesson to be learned here.
Joan: That variety is essential and that the best way to lose weight is to reduce portions eat a balanced diet and exercise?
Celia: Huh, that's funny, no we were thinking if we knew then what we know now we could've saved a ton of money on take-out. •*HW*•

Advice for the Modern Street Busker

By Diane Sokoloski

STREET BUSKING IS AN admirable occupation that looks good on a résumé. Anyone who suggests, no matter how truthful it may be, that you can not hold down a regular job, is woefully unaware of your resourcefulness of character and unique talents. By talent I mean something to do with the arts. A talent predicting which streetcar is full, or when your pasta is *al dente* is not suitable.

• Appearance can make or break the street busker. Ill-fitting clothing, from which a certain amount of body hair is visible, is a guarantee of low income.
• Remain at home if you have one, and play for your mother or pet, if you have one.
• You must be clean, well-groomed, and look like you just stepped down from a wedding cake. People will assume you are regularly employed and they will feel better about parting with their money. The ironic fact of life is, if you were gainfully employed as the musician or dancer that you are, you wouldn't be on the street in the first place.
• Location is important. Seek out places where economic activity is evident. Abandoned buildings, closed stores and empty fields do not constitute a financial district. Avoid the haggard working stiff and anyone with clenched fists. Depending on their level of self-esteem that day, they may feel it is your duty to serenade them at no cost.
• Evenings can work well if you choose your spot carefully. A popular upscale nightclub may yield some profitable results. A place that has broken windows or that smells like a litter box is not a good idea. Avoid biker bars or strip clubs where people are angry and frustrated. Most likely, after losing an arm wrestle or getting rebuffed by Buxom Brandy, the men leaving the establishment will not be in the mood to hear your soulful rendition of *Plaisir d'Amour*. You would be a beacon for their pent up anxiety and they may feel

compelled to show you their collection of switchblades and steel-toed boots. You have permission to use your cello or music stand as a shield or weapon.

• Season must be taken into consideration. Spring and summer months are best. You may try to do your act in January but it will be tough gathering an attentive crowd during a blizzard. Use common sense. A banjo solo will not sound very crisp with mittens on. Is it realistic to think that you can juggle those flaming rings during a hailstorm?

• At Christmas time stand close to the Salvation Army person. The ringing bell will attract people's attention, and they might think you're with the Sergeant. Take advantage of that giving spirit.

• Do not hang around elementary schools. You'll get a great crowd, but the youngsters will probably put dandelions, glittery stones and plastic dinosaurs in your money bucket. Local Block Parents will not hesitate to notify the police pedophile unit.

• Emergency areas of hospitals are a no-no. Unconscious people find it difficult to go into their pockets for money. Individuals with mental disorders may look at you nervously and get secret messages. Being loudly told that you are Beelzebub with your instrument of evil is not good for business.

• People with small pets are a possibility. Try a playful *How Much is that Doggie in the Window?* and the pet owner may even give Biffy the paper money to carry over and drop in your basket. Stay away from any dog whose neck and pectoral muscles are bigger than yours.

A rewarding career awaits those who follow these guidelines! •*HW*•

"Anyone who suggests, no matter how truthful it may be, that you can not hold down a regular job, is woefully unaware of your resourcefulness of character and unique talents."

Who Are the People in Your Village?

By Julie Ward

WE ALL KNOW THE expression "It takes a village to raise a child." Many of us are lucky enough to have an extended family of aunts, uncles, grandparents and close friends to help us raise, nurture and transmit our values to our children. But have you thought of inviting a new villager into your life, to give you a fresh perspective on common child-rearing problems? As the stories below illustrate, helpful villagers come from all walks of life.

Problem Child: The Potty Mouth

Carol S.'s second grader came home and said his best friends were no longer allowed to play with him because of his liberal use of swear words.

"My first reaction," she recalls, "was, 'Those kids can just go *$#@!* themselves. And so can their parents.' You know what I mean?"

Once she had calmed down, Carol was ready to tackle the job of helping her son make new friends.

"I knew that finding another group of little tattletales who can't wait to run home and tell mommy everything, even the obscenities, would be setting Johnny up for failure," Carol says. "You know what I mean?"

So she looked for a navy office nearby, or another place where sailors might hang out. Finding none and cursing her rotten luck, Carol took Johnny to the local truck stop.

"Truck stops are great," she says. "A lot of them have video arcades, and a lot of the truckers are hard core gamers. It's really nice when the kids and the truckers have something in common besides swearing. You know what I mean?"

Helpful Villager: The truckers and sailors (if you can find them) in your village can help The Potty Mouth feel less lonely.

Problem Child: The Bully

Most schools provide valuable support services to children who are bullied. It is not so easy to find help for the bully. Noted child-rearing expert/hypnotherapist Lucinda Maxwell would like to see that change. She offers a much-needed service to the bullies and parents in her community.

"Many people think bullies are aggressive and unafraid," she explains, "but bullies are the most fearful children you will ever meet. And what they fear most is change."

She offers parents this guided meditation to help their bully cope with the fear of things changing:

Imagine yourself all grown up. You are sitting at a big desk, in a corner office. You are happy. You are yelling at an unproductive worker. He trembles when you call him a useless fool. Oh look—here comes your assistant, with a latté for you. Look at your assistant while you yell at the unproductive worker. Both of them look really scared. You trip your assistant as he walks away from your desk. You've been tripping losers like him since elementary school.

Helpful Villager: The hypnotherapist in your village can prepare The Bully for a successful future in which things will stay pretty much the same.

Problem Child: The Little Spy

We all know that children can be traumatized when they see things they're not prepared for, from mom and dad engaging in sex, to the family tabby killing a bird, to leg warmers—in any decade, in any yarn, by any name. But there are some children who actually seek out the things we try to hide from them. These are the little spies.

The little spy is the neighbourhood kid who comes over to play, then sneaks upstairs and goes through your drawers while your own children coo over *Romper Room* and drink grape juice. The little spy smirks at you from behind the azaleas when the mail carrier comes to the back door with a "special delivery."

Is there anything the little spy does not want to see? In the 1950s, the existentialist/nutritionist/beat poet Crane Garibaldi stumbled upon the answer during a reading to an advanced meat safety class at the Sorbonne:

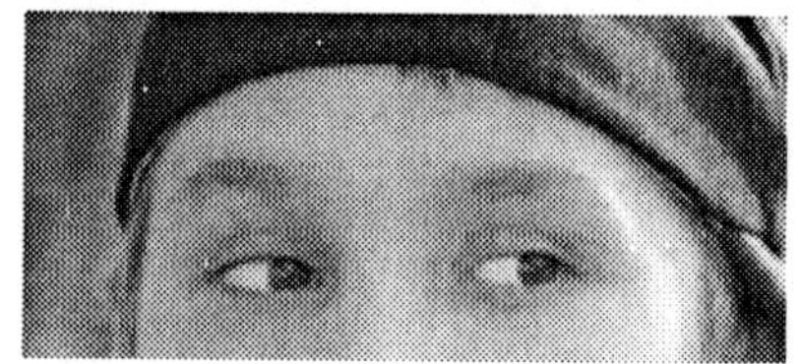

"Do maggots exist
under
a piece of rotten meat
If a s t r u n g o u t junkie
in a Left Bank whorehouse
doesn't turn it over and look
before
eating
it?
Maggots.

Milky writhing flesh-eating...wait a second...that's just what I need to scare those nosy French kids away from my naked Miles Davis pictures!"

Garibaldi's initial experiment with maggot-covered meat, naughty photos and French children from the working class was repeated in Europe, Japan and North America with uniform results. Follow up studies were conducted as well. In every case, the little spy was still minding his or her own business twenty years later.

Helpful Villager: The negligent food handler in your village can help you turn The Little Spy into a curiosity-free angel—and a vegetarian!

Three problem children, three solutions—no doubt there are countless other people in your village who can help you raise a better child. •*HW*•

Spring TV Preview!

Canadian Preview

By Sharon Grehan

CTV:

Signature series: Amanda Selnick Portrait of Courage. This emotionally charged two-hour drama based on the true story of Carpal Tunnel Syndrome survivor Amanda Selnick, details her trial and ultimate triumph over CTS with the help of her best friend Julie.

This story of love, courage and pain brought to you by the producers of *Danger at 24 Feet* and *Why Are My Feet So Cold?* is as heartbreaking as it is inspirational.

A hit at the International Festival for People Who Love Festivals and winner of the coveted Mercey Prize in the Movies Made for Under $100.00 category, this film is sure to become an instant classic.

"Powerful" —*John Smith*

"Must See." —*Jane Doe*

Canadian Broadcasting Company (CBC):

Cashing in on the past semi-successes of *Blackfly, History Bites, Back to Sherwood* and *The Broad Side* CBC is "thrilled and delighted to present our ground-breaking series: *History Sure Is Funny*. This half hour series features Canadian actors in knock down, roll on the floor, beat yourself about the head, hysterical, historical sketches." Asked how this show differs from the four other historical comedies the CBC cancelled, a spokesperson replied "It is completely different. I can give you a million examples for instance, the closing credits will be done in a Bodoni font and along with that we're making the CBC bug in the corner an eighth of an inch bigger."

Comedy Network:

Canada's premiere source of comedy for boys 9-14 is proud to present *Four Guys Scratch Themselves*.

Trevor, Buttfink, Sneeze and Zoe are couch potatoes in this zany half hour of ribald hilarity. With witty asides from their robot friend Scrote, this whacky quartet watch TV, drink, swear, talk about which girls they would "do" for a hundred bucks and yes, scratch themselves.

FGST has also spawned a preshow: *Two Guys Watch Four Guys Scratch Themselves* with Lloyd Roberstson.

Global TV:

CanWest committed to spend $83.4 million on original Canadian programming and thus far has invested over $25,000 dollars producing *Survivor Canadian Style*.

Based on the successful CBS series *Survivor*, Global's offering was meant to cash in on the Reality TV craze. Unfortunately there is a rumour the show may not make it to air. An insider reports: "It was a disaster. All but two of the contestants left before the first competition because it was cold and they were hungry and the two remaining refused to speak because they hadn't been introduced. We are editing our brains out but there is nothing there, nothing."

If the problems are not rectified by the April 7th air date, Global will run *Supermarket Checkout* the game show where contestants perform death-defying feats for $25 worth of groceries in the *Survivor Canadian Style* time slot.

The Women's Television Network:
And Then You Cry. Ellen McAndrew O'Toole hosts a weekly half hour show devoted to healing. Women from all over Canada** are encouraged to come on the show and spend the half hour weeping with sisters. Each week Ellen will speak in a soothing voice, nod understandingly, pat their hands and tell the women how brave they are.

This will be followed by *Talk About It* where the panellists discuss the panellists on the previous show.

The show also has an interactive element as there will be a live Internet feed so women at home can weep along with the panellists.

***except Newfoundland, New Brunswick, Alberta, Saskatchewan, PEI, Manitoba, Quebec and all three territories.*

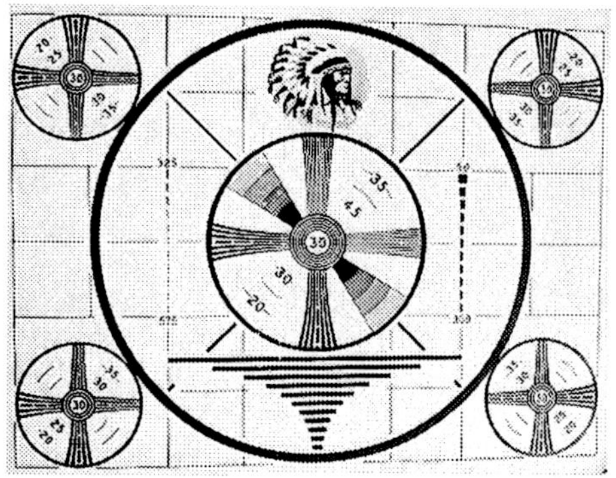

American Preview
By Elizabeth Hanes

With so much new drama, comedy, dramedy, and suspense about to take over the airwaves, you can't possibly know which shows will be worthwhile viewing. That's why we've done the hard part for you! Here are reviews of the major new offerings for the upcoming season.

NBC:
They took us inside the emergency room with *E.R.* They took us inside the White House with *West Wing*. Now, NBC takes us inside the seedy, action-packed world of the grocery store with: *Aisle 4*.

Meet Jake Murdoch, hunky manager and heir to the Pumpernickel Food Way chain of grocery stores. Feel the gut-churning tension as he calls for a "wet clean-up on Aisle 4." See the bagger Billy, Jake's nephew, make courtesy "deliveries" to certain female customers.

Shake your head at the off-colour antics of Dolly, the delicatessen manager, who routinely undercharges good-looking men. Hold your breath when Jake's wife, Sarah, announces over the store intercom that a customer needs assistance in the personal healthcare aisle. This gripping drama surely is "must-see TV" at its best!

ABC:
Searching desperately for a hit, and anxious to cash in on the reality TV craze, Disney-owned ABC has developed a sure-

fire winner: *The World of Diamond Slim.* In this wild, Seussian program, a tiny video camera is attached to the collar of Michael Eisner's painfully thin (but avowedly not anorexic) cat, Diamond Slim. Where she goes, you go! And, as it turns out, Mr. Eisner's neighbours were right: his cat goes constantly in their flowerbed.

William Shatner narrates the program, reading his own Dr. Seuss-inspired verse. One scene, for example, presents Slim peering up at a bird in Eisner's oak tree, while Shatner intones: "What's this I see, what can it be / Soon I'll scoot right up your tree / Then a featherless bird you'll be!"

You'll thrill to such family-oriented entertainment as Diamond Slim sleeping the day away under Mr. Eisner's desk. Slim upchucking a hairball on Mr. Eisner's plush bathroom carpeting. Slim getting vaccinated at the vet. Slim getting frisky with the tomcat next door. Yes, ABC finally has a major hit on its hands. Don't miss this one!

CBS:

The traditional home of heavy drama adds another serious contender to its stable. *The Education of Dax Mickford* stars Richard Dreyfuss portraying every character in every film he's ever been in. Dreyfuss plays, what else? a teacher in this, what else? uplifting story of a man who, what else? faces a crossroads in his life as he, what else? must re-assess his life in order to bring meaning to the chaos. You'll find yourself rooting for him as he copes with raising his, what else? headstrong daughter as a, what else? single father. As usual, Dreyfuss portrays Mickford as a, what else? slow-to-change man caught up in a, what else? constantly changing world. Fans of Dreyfuss won't want to miss this one!

PBS:

Finally realizing no one will ever pledge money to watch their network unless they provide exciting, entertaining, shallow fare, PBS adds a reality TV program to its fall lineup. *The Byronic Heroes* tracks eight teams of university graduate students as they race from England to Spain, then on to Portugal, Malta, Albania, and finally Greece, following the travels of George Gordon, Lord Byron.

At each stop in their journey, the teams face physical competitions. Teams that lose these challenges are eliminated from the game, until the two remaining teams compete in the championship challenge: a fight against the Turkish army. In addition to the physical tests, each team also must produce a 50-page critical essay exploring the evolution of the Byronic Hero from Childe Harold to Manfred.

Also thrown into the mix, to add excitement for the viewing audience, are impromptu events such as the "Don Juan" Round Robin, in which each member of a team must recite from memory one canto of the famous poem, while the next member picks up with the following canto in sequence. Hilarious stuff from sleep-deprived scholars! •*HW*•

Herstory: Searching For Mr. Right
By Sharon Grehan

READER JOANNE JACKSON'S steamy diary wins her a three pack of Clorets and a Swiffer duster. Well done, JJ!

June 4 – Well, he hasn't called but I'm pretty sure the construction on the street has knocked the phone lines out. Also, I blow dried my hair.

June 7 – Got a hang-up call today. I was pretty sure it was him and phoned him back. He claimed he didn't call, but it's hardly the kind of thing you're going to admit to is it? I think I woke him up because he didn't recognize my voice, or for that matter, my name. I told him I had free tickets to *Mamma Mia* on Saturday and he said he'd get back to me.

June 8 – Ticketmaster rejected my Visa, so I have to bring down a certified cheque for $150.00. Wow, do all shows cost that much or just the ones with music? My Mom is pretty pissed at me for cancelling out on my brother's wedding Saturday, but it's not as if I'm in the wedding party or anything, and it *is* his second wedding. I'll be at the church.

What do you wear to a show like that?

June 10 – Phoned him to find out what time we should meet and he said "For what?" He's so funny. It took me four hours to get from the church to the theatre. It's a good thing I left in the middle of the ceremony or I would have been late. God he's funny. When I woke him after the performance, he said it would have been better without all the singing. I laughed all the way home, the bus driver must have thought I was nuts.

I was hoping to have a drink afterwards, but he had to do laundry.

June 12 – I think there's something wrong with his answering machine, because I've left a message, well actually seven, and he hasn't called. I know he's there, because his car is outside. He lives in a gorgeous neighbourhood—it's so close it only takes me three buses!

If he had a dog, maybe I would run into him as he's walking it.

My mom is still not speaking to me.

June 13 – There was no answer at the door, but I saw the curtains move. I held the beagle's nose to the window. He was so surprised! I didn't know he had allergies, but it was great, we talked and talked, and I really felt in sync with him. Too bad his kettle was boiling dry.

June 14 – The Humane Society does not have an exchange or refund policy. They should really have a sign posted.

June 15 – I just got home!!!!!!!!!!! We finally DID IT!!!!!!!!!!!!! Last night I went to Spirits, a bar he always goes to. I walked in and tried to catch his eye, but he didn't see me. He was so surprised!! It was great, we talked and talked and he said, he's so funny, "Since it doesn't look like you're going you might as well sit down." I bought him eight pints and took him home in a cab. It was so wonderful—it wasn't just physical, we made a connection so deep it was scary. I know he was overwhelmed too, because when he woke up he just said "Oh, #&!$."

I'm so happy!

I vacuumed, reorganized his cutlery drawer and told him I'd be back later.

June 16 – I can't drink red wine. I really shouldn't have had the whole bottle, but it seemed such a waste. On the way over to his place, I picked up some things he needed like toilet paper, deodorant and a shoe tree, but there was no answer so I waited on the stoop.

Around ten his roommate Frank arrived and let me use the washroom. He's really sweet. I guess I shouldn't have opened the bottle, but by one a.m. the cold was really getting to me.

I don't know when I fell asleep, but I wish I hadn't vomited first.

June 17 – He wasn't at work when I dropped by. His neighbours are really nice though, one of them offered me a diet Coke. I think I'm going to like living in this area. Boy, is his roommate ever moody. He told me he would call the police if I kept calling. I think he's just jealous.

The beagle ate my dress shoes.

June 18 – I hid in the bushes by his house. He pulled up about two. As he was getting out of the car, I jumped out and yelled, "TA DA!!!!! I'm not wearing any underpants." I wish I had seen the girl before I yelled that last bit. Her name is Cheryl Hann—she seemed nice. Although he was with her I could tell he was yearning for me. I felt so sorry for her. She must have felt like a real loser.

I picked up my picnic basket, ice bucket, the beagle and caught the last bus home.

June 20 – His number's out of service and I don't know where he is. I've never seen anyone so frightened by their emotions. I found Cheryl's name in the phone book. I told her it was OK, and not to feel stupid or anything and maybe we could get together for dinner.

Wow is she a flake, she just laughed and hung up on me. I guess she just needs time. I read people pretty good.

June 21 – All my letters come back with "moved" on them. That's so weird because you think I would have seen a moving truck in his driveway.

It's a shame he didn't get the letters, but maybe it's for the best. I shouldn't have tried to end our relationship through the mail, but he's just too screwed up for me.

•*HW*•

"I vacuumed, reorganized his cutlery drawer and told him I'd be back later."

The 1-2-3 Guide to This Year's Hottest Hair Trend
By Crystal Click

THIS YEAR'S MEGA-TREND is a boon for busy women across the nation, nay the world. Ever pressed for time, today's woman has gone beyond the popular wash-and-wear styles of five minutes ago. Now they are to simply WEAR styles. The Wear is the millennium's answer to the Beehive, without the Aqua Net.

No longer will you have to slink repentantly into the hairdresser for an emergency "trim" after a 2 a.m. rendezvous with a bottle of Midol and a pair of kitchen shears. "Fix what?" she'll say.

Don't be surprised if people mistake you for a Hollywood megastar when they see you flitting around town with your new do. The man in your life will rejoice over your new freedom from the chains of hair entanglement. The day I came home with my Wear-do, my man said, "You didn't tell me you were going to the gym." My new look not only gave my spirits a lift, I must have looked thinner.

The Wear will work on any length hair. To achieve optimum results you need

A) natural wave
B) a home perm or
C) a vat of pine tar.

Step 1. This is the easy part. Abstain. No showers, no shampoo for at least a week. Good time to build that thatched hut you have been including on your list of things your really want to do this year. Natural oils are much better for your tresses and the environment, but if you have a pressing social event you can always apply a healthy smattering of petroleum jelly to your roots to speed up the process. Remember: less is only more if you are talking about physical labour.

Step 2. Late in the evening, on the day your hair is at peak lubrication, thoroughly wet it with imported mineral water (preferably one that tastes like a mixture of acetaminophen and aluminum foil, the more minerals, the less flexible the hair shaft becomes). You may blot out the excess water with a towel.

Step 3. While hair is still very damp, to bed you go to let the Sand Man do his magic. Actually, it is the tossing and turning that manufacture the highly aesthetic lack of volume and uneven waves but if you are unhappy with the result a good handful of sand WILL add texture and sparkle.

For a fetching night-time look, tie hair in a high pony tail with left over yarn from any of the forty yarn inclusive projects you started and didn't finish in your crafty stage. Then, emulsify eight teaspoons of 100% organic opossum guano by rubbing your palms together in the fashion of self-seeking gold diggers. Work this mixture through your locks and arrange the free strands Stein-esquely (Think Albert Ein or Bride of Franken). You are now ready for an evening of dinner and dancing or a friendly game of rugby. You are guarantied to look just as fresh when the evening ends as you did when you arrived at the event.

Deceptively simple in nature, the Wear-do transcends all cultural barriers. It is the official hair style of the USA's 2005 delegates to Fashion Victims for Peace and has been voted Best Style of the Year by Four Ladies Who Ride Really Big Motorcycles and Chew Tobacco. •*HW*•

HW DISPATCH: News for Happy Women

Anthrax Scare At Fashion Show

Police were called backstage to Penelope Philthrop Theatre after a messenger reported seeing a powdery substance on a dressing table.

Superintendent Alan Chancer said they received a report at 7 p.m. that a suspicious powder was spotted on a mirror next to a razor blade. Unfortunately, police were unable to test the substance as one of the coordinators of the event panicked and flushed it down the toilet before police arrived.

Reporter Sal Ventura who was covering the event for *Women's Wear Daily* said that the mood was surprisingly upbeat. "Most people, when told that they may have been exposed to anthrax would be distraught, but not these women. They were inspirational."

The models declined to be tested for exposure stating that they were "fine, just fine," and that they'd "just like to get on with the show."

Ventura found their bravery moving. "I think they set a great example for all of us." —*S. Grehan*

Children's Game Goes Wrong, Proves Adage

Ten-year-old Tommy Mahew had the unfortunate honour of proving correct the timeless maternal adage "Sure, it's funny until someone loses an eye" when he sustained a suction cup dart injury during a game of cops and robbers Saturday afternoon. Wearing a white gauze bandage over his left eye, Tommy shook his head sadly and told reporters, "We were having a lot of fun until this happened. I should have listened to Mom." Having now been scientifically proven, the vision safety maxim, repeated by mothers throughout the centuries, joins other timeless axioms in the mother's arsenal, such as "Eat your vegetables; they're good for you" and "No one ever died from taking a bath." —*E.Hanes* •*HW*•

The Rules of Family: Advice from Donna Corleone

By Pamela Monk

DEAR MADRONE,

My husband and I have been together for a long time, and he has always been kind, never cheated, doesn't beat me. He makes a good living. But he wants to move, for a promotion, to another state. On the one hand, it would be a come up for him, a classier operation than the one he is in now, a pay raise, more respect from certain quarters that matter to him. On the other hand, we have a very nice set up here, my friends and family are near and I have a good job. There is no such promise if I move. He says he wants me to be happy, and I won't be happy if I move. But I won't be happy if we don't move and he isn't happy. This whole thing is driving us both *pazzu*. What can you tell me?

Not wanting to spoil a good thing,

Fort Lee

Dear Wanting,

This is a half dozen of one, six of the other thing. How you've been is a good indication of how you will be, though not always. Can he stay with a gracious heart? Can you go with one? If one of you can come up with the right attitude you will be fine, no resentment. If neither of you can, then your marriage is in trouble, I am sorry to say, no matter how good your jobs or where you live. If you can move without resentment do so. If you cannot, take the heat up front, because it's going to come round and bite you, guarantee. One thing to keep in mind, a good provider who neither cheats nor beats could belong in a museum for display.

God bless, Donna.

Chapter Four – April

Cruise Couture
By Jessica Becht

A GENERATION OR TWO ago, crossing the Atlantic aboard a palatial ocean liner was a luxury reserved for the moneyed class. In our time, however, stigma-free second mortgages have democratized the travel industry. Leisurely ocean voyages are no longer the especial preserve of the elite. Yet, the fabled glamour of yesteryear too often intimidates the modern traveller. Miss Middle America may even pass up a yearned for world tour, fearing her tatty wardrobe might provoke a sound snubbing from apocryphal snobs Mrs. Moneybags and Sir Spendalot.

Like any sophisticate, the typical American miss has snivelled over *Titanic* and slumped in a catatonic slaver before umpteen re-runs of *The Love Boat*. Bemused, she dithers over whether to stuff her steamer trunks with Edwardian corsets or alluring polyester gowns. In truth, both options are passé and an unassuming new aesthetic prevails. The motto of today's modish traveler is Careless Comfort.

So, gird your loins with fanny packs and prepare to set sail! The following fundamentals will swathe you in an aura of slapdash glamour to rival any seven seas Siren.

Traditionally, the pinnacle of your shipboard wardrobe would be a formal evening ensemble. Clad in finery, old-fashioned cruisers commemorated the final night of their journey with a Captain's Dinner. Before fretting that Wal-Mart lacks an evening gown department, remember that the concept of formality has grown slack as a beer-swiller's belly in recent years. While "white tie" once decreed tiaras and tailcoats, nowadays such dictums may be flouted in favour of barefaced sloth. No need to invest in a fuddy-duddy gown when your trusty sweats can be gussied up with a Be-Dazzler and some subtle alterations to the neckline. Such expansive attire will accommodate your dessert bar dabblings, and prove practical for after-dinner dancing, when you can look forward to a rousing conga line rather than executing dull, outdated tangos and fox trots.

Shipboard bathing in the solarium is another essential cruise activity. Decades ago, a lady would don an elaborate bathing costume before permitting a single pedicured toe to peep over the threshold of her suite. Only after careful accessorizing, encompassing sandals to bathing cap, was she set for a demure dip. Such complicated rituals have thankfully evanesced. A contemporary bathing beauty requires only a simple string bikini. This universal item flatters all figure types, showcasing both the ribs of the gaunt and the swells of the corpulent with equal zeal.

Though you may sunbathe by day, evenings at sea are often chill. A lady of yore might have snuggled in mink during that tipsy moonlit stroll with the brilliantined fortune hunter her parents always warned about. As he inclined to whisper saccharine nullities, her paramour would have estimated a crude net worth by the heirlooms glittering against her lobes. "A bit out of my league", you sniff, resigning yourself to another vacation spent sipping expired beer in your basement. Such wretchedness is uncalled for. By feigning a charming laxity regarding credit card receipts, you too can lure a calculating adventurer. Only a little ingenuity is required to mimic the look of a plutocrat. Unscrew a few light bulbs before flaunting your gumball-machine bargains with aplomb. And as a modern bombshell of limited means, you might try fashioning the *de rigueur* furs from hapless yet striking roadkill.

Shipboard bathing in the solarium is another essential cruise activity.

In bygone days, the leisured set went in for a snappy bumper of bridge by evening, affording well-dressed ladies occasion to display elegant décolleté gowns. As only the most antique citizens can still distinguish a trick from a trump suit, cruise directors promote alternate entertainments. Swap the décolleté gown for a halter-top, and try your luck at another game of skill, such as video poker.

Barring a severe bout of dysentery, you will not spend your entire voyage afloat. Don't neglect to pack several pairs of abbreviated shorts. Ladies of yesteryear toured world capitals in sedate linen dresses, but such priggish frumpery hardly presents Americans as the carefree, egalitarian, and sensuous people the viewers of dubbed *Baywatch* episodes have come to expect. A capacious handbag will help carry ashore the essential passport, camera, guidebook, toilet paper, and carton of cigarettes.

So Miss Middle America, the next time Duchesse Cruise Lines crams your mailbox with unsolicited advertorials extolling the splendors of an Axis of Evil world tour, don't let your unsightly wardrobe keep you at home. The seaweedy depths of your laundry basket should yield duds suitable for a most memorable cruising experience. •*HW*•

A Day in the Life of Martha Stewart

By Sharon Grehan

OUR INTREPID celebrity interviewer Libby Zimmerman was not able to snag an interview with this ex-con homemaker extraordinaire but the resourceful Libby *was* able to gain entry to Martha's lair, a sumptuous 153 acre estate, under the guise of settling a personal injury suit.

Once inside Martha's home Libby "borrowed" a page from Martha's day-timer and a ramekin.

Martha Stewart: A Day In The Life

4:00 Wake up, dress (note to self: buy more blue shirts).

4:10 Spray bangs.

4:45 Bang pots to wake up roosters.

5:00 Workout. Treadmill, 3 mile run, 350 sit ups 212 push-ups.

5:12 Mow 153 acres with power mower, fix engine.

7:00 Breakfast: hover over cook as she prepares truffle omelette. Criticize.

7:30 Crank call ex husband.

8:00 Corner Poncho market.

8:30 Tape show. Prepare Beef Wellington with Ma, Walnut Blue Cheese Coins and Pink Heart cookies. Rewire a lamp, create Fortuny inspired lace tablecloth and build under the bed storage box.

12:00 Tell mother that she won't work in this town again.

12:30 Lunch: Bologna sandwich.

12:45 Call ex and hang up.

12:48 Call daughter and tell her about bobby pin in the Louis XVI night table. Ask if it belongs to her.

13:00 Drive to Omnimedia while dictating new book. Detour past ex's house six times.

14:45 Say no to every proposal submitted by board members. Rephrase their ideas as own.

16:00 Don floppy hat and check K-Mart for product placement. Have shelf-stacker fired.

16:30 Drive past ex's house.

17:00 Write script for next day's taping.

17:01 Teach cats to sing.

17:35 Sit in Suburban with binoculars and scout for trespassers.

18:00 Call daughter and ask her if she knows where nail file is.

18:45 White glove test in furnace room after dinner.

18:30 Create new colours and think about getting all rights to red.

18:40 Fire drill.

18:45 Call daughter and ask if she phoned. Make up something about being in the shower.

18:48 Have 4 pizzas sent to ex.

19:00 Whip up a night cream out of mayonnaise and egg shells.

19:20 Bedtime.

19:30 Call ex and hang up.

•*HW*•

Your Grout Could Be Killing You!

The latest home hazard.

By Sharon Grehan

A SPECIAL REPORT commissioned by the Committee for Special Reports released their scientific findings on grout yesterday and the results are startling!

Epoxy resin also known as grout (pronounced 'gr-owt' or 'gr-oot' if you are Canadian) used to hold ceramic tiles in place presents the following health hazards:

- Adverse eye effects like conjunctivitis and corneal damage
- Skin irritation
- Known to release hazardous vapours

If you are laughing up your sleeve because you chose cement grout - think again. Improperly treated cement grout can become a medium for Bacteria which of course leads to death and overweight sedentary smokers with ceramic tile in their homes suffered high incidences of lung cancer, diabetes and heart disease!

Sobering Facts

- 99% percent of all bathrooms with ceramic tiles in homes built after 1960 have grouting.
- 99% percent of all bathrooms with ceramic tiles in homes built before 1960 have a significant amount of grout.
- It affects women 30 times more than men and is therefore more serious.

What You Can Do:

- Avoid setting your ceramic tiles on fire.
- Try not to work with uncured grout every day.
- Refrain from scraping the dirt off the grout with your fingernail and resist the urge to taste it.

Renowned activist Renee Heller: "When I found out these results I was appalled. I'm home-schooling my children because their classroom was toxic, I've forbidden apples because of Alar, we threw out our cell phone and electric blankets because of EMF's, got rid of our aluminum cookware while we are still able to remember to do so and now this? How do we keep our children safe?"

Heller has started an Azure Ribbon Campaign to put an end to the madness.

A spokesperson for the Public Safety Commission, Merle Eleanor Luck, was questioned about this alarming report.

"Yes it is true that epoxy resin can release hazardous fumes, but you would have to burn it, and I don't really understand why someone would do that. You would only experience eye and skin irritation after repeated exposure to uncured epoxy and improperly treated cement grout. I mean every day for years. Yes, it *can* harbour bacteria, but you would have to actually *ingest* large quantities of it for it to present a significant risk."

That is where women are most at risk states activist Heller. "Women are more inquisitive, so they are more likely to eat grout than men are.

"I've removed all grout from my home. It has been a sacrifice because the tiles don't stay up as well without it, but I'll do anything for my family." •*HW*•

Making a Profit While Making Babies

By SB Shoemaker

YOU'VE BEEN PUTTING it off for ages. All that inconvenience, the mess and – oh, the expense! Having a bundle of joy used to mean dropping a bundle of cash, but not anymore.

Welcoming a new baby into your home is easier and cheaper than ever before with the exclusive Bargain Baby Sponsor System® used for years by celebrities like Catherine Zeta-Jones and Anna Nicole Smith and now available for the first time to the public.

The kit comes complete with everything you need, including sperm, pregnancy test, calendar, and sponsor list with cross referenced chart for tracking each one. Just mark the calendar with your due date the instant the little plastic stick is dry (remember to wash your hands first!). Then pick up your phone and start to dial.

In a few minutes, you can regain the peace of mind most parents sacrifice for at least eighteen years. Selling rights to your child's future makes soundproofing the nursery affordable, allowing you the full eight hours of peace and quiet every night that you deserve.

Been eyeing that $2,500, hand-crafted Balmoral Pram but didn't want to waste the money on someone who's just going to grow out of it anyway? Now you don't have to! Plan ahead for octuplets, then the manufacturer will happily give you at least one. All you have to do is tattoo one letter on each baby's darling Buddha belly, then have them photographed for the ad campaign. An elegant free stroller and a picture worth a lifetime of memories: what could be better! And don't stop at the belly – your baby's soft skin has room for hundreds of endorsements – more than enough to cover that diamond-studded Gucci diaper bag and handcrafted Versace crib with matching changing table and dresser. You won't care when they get slimed with baby drool – or worse – if you're not paying for them.

The BBSS® is easy to use and limited only by your creativity. Start by building your own website, where you can post updates (sick again this morning!) and your ultrasound pix. Gerber, Huggies, and Johnson & Johnson will be fighting for the chance to be your official sponsors with links on your site.

Next, invite the local TV news team into your delivery room to share your joy. Leading distributors of educational films to schools, universities and Lamaze classes are happy to pick up the tab for your hospital stay in exchange for the rights to use the film. This also offers numerous opportunities for product placement, as you casually sip a name brand soft drink in between contractions.

The BBSS® shows you how to keep your privacy while going public. Assuming a lack of distinctive scars, all women look the same from the waist down while giving birth. Just keep the camera pointed where the action is. A bonus benefit: your doctor will gladly waive his fee when his name is prominently printed on your inner thighs, displayed to an unlimited number of potential new patients. If you pick someone straight out of med school or rebounding from a malpractice claim, he might also pay you cash to do it!

Make sure you plan ahead for the perfect moment to give birth. The most lucrative time to deliver is 12:01 a.m. on January 1st, guaranteeing your appearance on the local news and additional chances to plug your sponsors.

It also helps to have a litter. Have you noticed how easily mothers of multiples manage? That's because they've used this system for years. When you have 6 or 7 or more babies at once, manufacturers of baby products enter a frenzied bidding war for the privilege of giving you lots of stuff, including buses and new homes.

An additional feature included in the BBSS® (at no extra charge!) is the packet that contains everything you need to sell the right to name your baby on eBay for the highest possible price. Think how exciting those final minutes of the auction will be, waiting to see if your child will be Phillip Morris or Daimler Chrysler.

Later, you can dress him in a sleeper decorated with a colourful print of beer logos, and tuck him in for the night, content in the knowledge that, with the BBSS®, your financial future has been secured. •*HW*•

Beauty 911
By Elize Bergeron

Q: I'm a forty-five year old woman and I love to keep up with the latest trends. Recently after wearing pigtails and a midriff-baring top a friend of mine pulled me aside to tell me that what I was wearing was too young for me that it was time to grow-up and dress more "age-appropriate." I was completely destroyed by this comment. What should I say to her?

A: Some people would say that you should not let your friend's advice bother you. We live in an age where a person should be free to wear what they want when they want, that we are individuals and should be free to express our personality through our hair and makeup as well as our style of dress.

Those people are, of course, crazy. If they are right, then why aren't we seeing old crumblies like you on the cover of *Vogue*? No my dear, it's time to start facing facts. You are past your sell-by date and it's time to move on to tasteful knee length frocks, slacks and perhaps a few scarves for zest.

As far as what you should say to your friend, how about a simple, humble "Thank you."

Q: I have very brittle nails, what can I do to strengthen them?

A: The nails, like very other part of the body, have muscles that need to be toned and exercised on a normal basis. These simple tips will turn your nails from brittle bitties to tender talons!

1. Balance a pencil on the edge of your nails and do 16 lifts.
2. Placing your fingers (tips first on the desk) push up. Repeat 46 times.
3. Acknowledge that they may have a problem.
4. For the nail cardio hold right arm straight over a table, tuck all fingers in save index and middle fingers. Place these on the table and make then run. Once you are comfortable with this action, repeat the steps with the left arm until the left hand is chasing the right. (You may wish to tie yourself to a chair as this activity can be quite frenetic). Incorporate the other fingers by wiggling them.

Do this exercise for 15 minutes every morning and for an hour and 3 seconds every evening.

Before you go to bed apply a paste of mashed avocado and slip on some white Egyptian cotton gloves.

Avoid any activity that requires your hands. •*HW*•

Happy Woman's Guide to Frugal Living

By Elizabeth Hanes

WITH TAX SEASON breathing hotly down our necks, it's a good time to review smart money management principles. After all, a happy woman is a wealthy woman, and even the average girl can amass a fortune with some simple money-saving ideas and practices.

First, learn to save money from your regular household budget.

- Fire your live-in personal chef and start eating out at every meal. *Projected savings:* $14,000 a year.
- Reduce ATM fees by simply withdrawing all the cash from your husband's chequing account once a month. *Projected savings:* $400 a month.
- Downgrade from the "Endowed Member" level of Fine Arts Centre membership to the "Sustaining Member" level. *Projected savings:* $5,000 a year.
- Sell your theatre season tickets for the shows you don't want to attend, like that tiresome *Pirates of Penzance* they insist on staging every year. *Projected savings:* $545 per season.
- Eliminate expensive dental bills by pulling all your teeth out and getting fitted for dentures. *Projected savings:* $3,800 over your lifetime.
- Eliminate the custom scenting feature from your dog grooming service. *Projected savings:* $48 a month.
- Stop dry cleaning your clothes! A far better strategy is to wear your dry-cleanables once, donate them to charity, deduct the value from your taxes, and buy new clothes. *Projected savings:* varies, depending on your clothing budget, but at least $10,000 per year.
- Take up chinchilla ranching and make your own furs. Not only money-saving, but a fun hobby! *Projected savings:* $6,500 a year.
- Negotiate with your vendors to add value to their services without increasing your cost, thereby getting you more "bang for the buck." For example, inform your pool boy, Garibaldi, that he'll need to service you, or rather the pool, twice as often if he wishes to maintain his staff position.

Now that you have some "mad money" in your pocket, you need to learn how to turn it into even more money. Try one or all of these strategies.

- Buy real estate. Decrepit, old downtown office buildings that can be renovated into trendy nightclubs are exceptionally good buys.
- Buy stocks. It's easy, and there's no need to do much research. Just pick some companies you like, such as Montgomery Ward, or any of the so-called "tech" stocks and plow your money into shares. Soon, you'll be a millionaire!
- Create your own non-profit organization. This is one of the best

ways to make money fast! Just think of a social concern you can address (such as relocating park pigeons to the wild), and start raising funds. It's that easy!

- Get in on the "ground floor" of a new multi-level marketing scheme.

These golden economic times won't be with us forever. A smart girl knows to save up her "egg money" for a rainy day. With these strategies, and many more that any clever girl can think up, you'll have plenty of money in your safe deposit box to flee the country when the IRS audits you. So don't be a goose – get started on saving up your golden egg today! •*HW*•

Herstory: I Hate My Thighs!!!

By Sharon Grehan

An anguished account from faithful HW reader Jessica McBride. Jessica 33 of Stockton, is the lucky winner of a brand new Ford Aerostar key chain.

I GUESS I'VE ALWAYS had a love-hate relationship with my thighs. Even as a girl I knew I needed them but I didn't know why there had to be so much of them.

For the most part through my twenties I could ignore them except when I was sweaty and sat on vinyl.

The first time I noticed a major change was when I wore silk pants for the first time at an office Christmas party. I was strolling to the bar and detected a soft whisper as my thighs rubbed together.

It wasn't obvious unless you told everyone to shut up and listen so I stopped doing that. I didn't pay too much attention until a few days later when I was walking to the bus.

I was wearing jeans and the swish, swish sound became more and more evident until I realized my thighs were trying to communicate with me!

It was mostly small talk at first: the weather, the state of the transit system, but as days passed and I changed pants the voice became more insistent.

Little suggestions like "why don't you run for the bus" changed to "why don't you run in front of the bus".

I knew I was in trouble when a particularly malevolent pair of Capri pants encouraged me to audition for *Bring in da Noise, Bring in da Funk.*

I sought help but could not hear the therapist over the sarcastic murmurings of my linen trousers. I tried wearing skirts and dresses but that didn't work because then the pantyhose would make fun of my hair.

One night I couldn't sleep because my pajamas wanted to watch *Late Nite.* Fed-up and depressed I threw on some clothes and went for a walk.

The night was cold so I nipped into my neighbourhood McDonalds for coffee and a muffin. As I sat down to eat, my trousers started nagging me about my caffeine intake and my calcium deficiency. I was tired and felt I could take no more. I raised the cup with unsteady hands and the steaming contents poured into my lap.

The pain was literally searing. I have a blurred remembrance of my thighs' anguished screams and images of the wait staff anxiously hovering and pointing out the "Caution: Contents Hot" warning on the cup.

Then silence.

Pain—a lot of pain.

But silence. Complete silence.

I was free.

Once again I was able to walk the streets without being told to trip an old woman or steal newspapers. Freedom lovely freedom!

There has been the odd murmur from my thighs since then especially when corduroy is involved but the minute I venture near those glorious arches the murmurs turn to silence.

My life would be perfect if only my feet would stop humming *Wipe Out* off key. •*HW*•

My Triumph Over Canker

By Britney Spears, as told to Elizabeth Hanes

Recently, I had a chance to sit down with pop diva Britney Spears to chat about her recent bout with canker. Here is her story, as best I could make it out from the garbled cassette tapes.

I FIRST NOTICED the symptoms while I was on stage in Allentown, Pennsylvania. Suddenly, in the middle of singing one of my classics *Oops, I Did It Again*, I noticed a tingling sensation inside my lower lip. Of course, the show must go on, so I sang through the pain.

The next morning, I started to chug down my breakfast Pepsi and, whoa! The burning was unreal! It felt like this little spot inside my lip was on fire. I asked the tour medics to look at it, but they couldn't find anything. I wasn't comfortable with that diagnosis, so I flew to California to see my internist. She couldn't find anything wrong, either.

My feminine intuition told me something was going on, however. I knew I was sick. I just wasn't sure how sick. One thing was for sure, though: I wasn't going to stop until I had a diagnosis.

I cancelled my next scheduled tour date in Tallahassee in order to fly to New York City for a consultation with an oncologist. By now, the pain was excruciating, and my lip was starting to swell up, as if a bee had stung me or something. Although, of course, I mean, I knew it wasn't that!

The oncologist was booked solid with A-list celebrities, so she referred me to a top-notch ear-nose-and-throat doctor instead. I had an hour to kill before the appointment, so I had them close Macy's to the public while I did some shopping. New shoes always make a girl feel better!

By the time I got into the doctor's exam room, my lip definitely was swollen and raw. Still, I wasn't prepared for the diagnosis. I mean, is anyone ever ready to hear "that" word?

When the ear-nose-throat doctor said, "Britney, you've got canker," I started to cry. I was just so stunned. I didn't think young people got canker. I thought the disease only struck old people or the very unlucky. I certainly didn't think that I, a young wealthy person, could get it. I was afraid I might never be able to sing again.

Thank goodness I'd brought my mother and two of my best friends with me to the appointment. I was numb from shock after the doctor's pronouncement and barely heard the rest of the conversation. Something about "aphthous ulcer" and "no usual treatment." I was scared to death!

My friends took lots of notes, though.

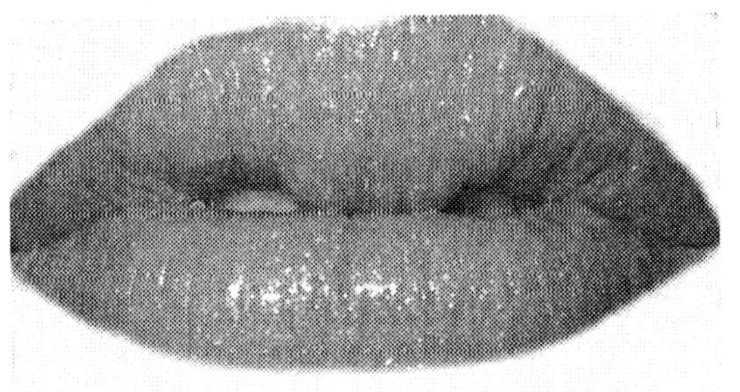

"I mean, is anyone ever ready to hear 'that' word?"

Evidently a mouth sore like the one I had is the most common form of canker. The doctor said it would clear up on its own within a few weeks. She also said something about "a big baby" and "spoiled brat," but like I said, nothing really registered because of my shock.

The doctor recommended I put ice on the canker or dab on some Ora-Jel. After several days of treatment, I noticed a significant reduction in swelling, and the pain had almost disappeared. Luckily, I've been able to return to a normal life. And, yes, I can still sing!

I cherish every day now. My husband Kevin Federline and I have become much closer. He is my number one supporter. He makes sure I go to my follow-up visits with the doctor and keeps Ora-Jel on hand in the first aid kit on the tour bus, just in case I have a relapse. I don't know what I'd do without him. I wish everyone who suffers from this terrible disease could have someone as good-looking as Kevin to take care of them.

Not really.

Mainly, I just want to encourage everyone to listen to their body. Don't let doctors tell you there's nothing wrong with you when there is. Trust your instincts. Early diagnosis is crucial in dealing with something as serious as canker. Be healthy! •*HW*•

HW DISPATCH:
News for Happy Women

Soy Drinks A "Terrorist Plot"

STARBUCKS EMPLOYEE Chad Templeton turned in his smock Saturday after serving yet another soy chai latté "Don't you people know this whole soy thing is, like, a terrorist plot?" he raved at customers waiting politely. "And what the hell is 'chai,' anyway?" A company veteran, with 15 hours of service to his credit, Templeton was escorted outside, where he was eager to speak to reporters, if only any had been available. In light of the frenzied media absence, Templeton announced to no one in particular that he thought he'd "go home and watch TV." —*E.Hanes*

Chad Templeton: "What the hell is chai?"

Model rejects Darwinian Theory

Supermodel Vim called a press conference Tuesday to officially announce her rejection of Darwinian Theory. "I think that ape stuff is stupid."

Asked if she was a Creationist she said "No, I'm a Hungarian but that's irregardless."

Dr. Edmond Forester, spokesperson for the Lower Poughkeepsie Scientific community was quoted as saying "I guess it's back to the drawing board."

Vim looked radiant in a black slit-to-the-waist Katayone Adeli one piece and a pair of Alexander McQueen's knee-high boots, topping the ensemble with a Gucci oblong handbag. Her boyfriend, swimmer turned model-turned producer Brock Lasalle supported Vim during the 15 second conference and vowed to stand by her. —*S.Grehan*

The Rules of Family: Advice from Donna Corleone

By Pamela Monk

DEAR MADRONE:
My mother in law constantly criticizes my house keeping, and my husband will not take my part. She makes me feel like a *babbo*. The other day, she came over for dinner, but before she sat down to eat, she ran a vacuum around the house, and did a load of laundry, ironed the sheets, made the bed, then cleaned the water tank in the upstairs toilet, and swept out the leaves and dust from the garage. All the while she was rolling her eyes and reminding my husband that he deserved the best. He has no intention of speaking to her about his, it's his mother, I understand. Other than that with my husband I have no beef.
Sign me stunada, from Pyramus

Dear Stunada:
The way I see it, you got two choices. You can submit, she is the *capo di tutti capo*, and no one should get between a person and his mother, that's how it is, wait your turn, one day she'll die. Or you can take to the mattress and have her whacked, of course, the only way this can be done is in secret and by your own children. Which keeps everything right.
God bless, Donna.

Chapter Five – May

Bovine Metabolism Diet

By Crystal Click

AFTER A LITERALLY ground-breaking 8 day study performed by the North Washougal Institute for Adiposity, Dr. Kristina Sveltendski has released an eating plan that is sweeping the country. In the three short months since Dr. Sveltendski announced her findings to the American Council of Pompous Overpaid Individuals, thousands of women have gone from portly to pretty. Bovine to Divine. The basis of the Bovine Metabolism Diet is so simple you may have heard it already. The story behind it is so fascinating you will want to hear it again and again.

Formerly a stoutness management psychotherapist, Sveltendski was intrigued when patient after patient made references to cattle when describing their weighty issues. As you well know, the bovine kind are famous for their excessive abdomens, wide hips and sagging mammary glands. Dr. Sveltendski grew increasingly concerned as the corpulent-cow and upholstered-urban-woman connection played out in her mind.

"My hypothesis was, if it makes Ol' Bess a big fat cow, it will make Jennifer or Jane or Kelly a big fat cow. Birds of a feather all spread together so I knew there was something physiological causing the girls to marble up."

After milking the existing body of data, Dr. Sveltendski projected a correlation between the rise and fall of bovine metabolism and the foods they ingest. In six months, she had solicited enough grants to paper a padded cell.

Kristina's "Bovine Dining" project, as it was dubbed by her staff began in a rural Wyoming farming community. The study included a ~~whopper~~, whopping total of 9,000 Guernseys, Jerseys and Herefords. Animals were imported from 6 continents. A control group of 3,000 cows were kept on their regular plant based diets of greens and whole grains mimicking USDA food pyramid. Three thousand were fed powdered diet drinks twice a day patterned after the nutritional regimen of such woodland creatures as the gazelle and a generation of moss-like plants. The final three thousand were fed a diet tailored to match the food intake of various lean carnivorous animals. This feeding plan including whole chickens and live squirrels.

Each cow was meticulously weighed and measured on day one and day eight. To the amazement of Dr. Svelt's staff, the control group not only failed to maintain their weight, they collectively gained 4,500 pounds. Clearly the plant-based diet was wreaking havoc on the delicate metabolism of our participants.

Only thirteen of the protein shake cows made it to day eight. By day four, 50% were wearing belted trousers ranging from two to four sizes too small and tucking in their Lycra tops to show off their new figures. By day six, 90% had bleached their hair and run off with new studs they had met online. By all accounts, Dr. Sveltendski and staff cannot recommend the powdered drink mixes to any creature, much less humans, with taste buds or taste for that matter. In any case, the weight loss was questionable. When the wayward cattle sent in before and after photos, the only differences noted by Dr. Sveltendski's staff were the now smiling expressions and the flexed abdominal muscles.

Finally, group number three was weighed and measured. Victory! The raw protein group didn't just maintain they lost a total of 6,972 lbs.! The climax is best relayed in Dr. Sveltendski's own words:

"When the cows were weighed there was murmur of disbelief among some of the younger members of our staff. So I called Wendy McQueen, the head of our feeding department to verify the authenticity of our results.

"Not only did Wendy verify the results, she sent up another shock for the day. One hundred percent of our previously super size eaters in group three exhibited a rapid drop in appetite after the very first live squirrel (which we admittedly had to force feed many of them). When the chicken carcasses were laid out the next morning not a single cow ventured forth. By changing their diets from cellulose plant based products to raw and/or living protein, we accomplished hunger management, a 100% turnaround in the BMI of the entirety of the bovine group three population and we came in several thousand dollars under budget."

"Clearly the plant-based diet was wreaking havoc on the delicate metabolism of our participants."

"The concept is so basic I am forgoing the usual book deals and rights exclusivity of my findings and freely proclaiming: If you look like a cow, then you are probably eating like one. In conclusion, I have three words meat, meat, meat. The fresher the better. Chicken tartare, sushi, sweet and sour pork *au naturel.* The world is a grassy meadow and you don't have to eat it."

Dr. Kristina, now weighing 87 lbs. after following her own diet, neglected to mention an added benefit to living the NeoBovine way. If you choose the all natural approach and harvest your own forest creatures as opposed to ordering them pre-packaged from Sveltco, you will enjoy the added benefits of a cardiovascular workout. Each year or two a diet phenomenon hits the country by storm. This one hits the broad side of the barn. Give it a try. •*HW*•

Funeral Etiquette Dos & Don'ts
By Sharon Grehan

What Sassy lassie doesn't want to make a splash at a passing? These easy to follow tips will keep you from making a fearsome funeral faux pas and make you belle of the burial!

Don't attend funerals of people you don't know.
Don't try to outdo the family's grief.
Don't use the occasion to "schmooze."
Don't videotape the service.
Don't ask for "just a peek-a-doodle" if it is a closed casket.
Don't rate the funeral with a 1-10 scale in front of the family.
Don't race the hearse to the cemetery.
Do offer your help, but *Don't* charge for it.
Don't make statements like "something seems fishy to me," or "I hope they did an autopsy."
Don't remark that the deceased looks "way better than they ever did."
Don't sit in the front row of the church and lean over the seat to wave at everyone you know coming in.
Do realize that the grieving family probably knew the deceased better than you did.
Don't approach the widow/widower and ask for the fifty dollars the deceased owed you.
Don't make an offer to the widow/widower on the deceased's clothes.
Don't climb on headstones to get a better view.
Don't do impressions of the deceased.
Don't ask about the "eats" the minute you arrive at the funeral home.
Don't use the word "rooked" if a discussion of funeral expenses arises.
Don't ask the widow/widower on a date at the funeral home.
Don't tell everyone how much your flower arrangement cost and offer to show them the bill if they don't believe you.
Don't remove anything from the coffin as a memento.
Don't tell the grieving family "it could be worse" and then go into a long rambling story about the passing of your little dog Blue.
Don't tell the relatives that this is the smallest funeral you've ever seen.
Don't use a fake name like "I.P. Nightly" in the guestbook.
Don't offer to make a beer-run. •*HW*•

Don't *race the hearse to the cemetery.*

How to Get Eyes Worth Eyeing

By Christina Delia

THE SECRET TO KEEPER peepers lies in one, glamorous word: makeup. Yes, *lies*. The wisest of women have been lying about the important things for years (namely age and hair colour, although this writer once knew a smart surgeon named Bertha who graduated at the top of her class and now operates under the moniker Doctor Lola X. McBambi.)

Remember that men like sexy women, but they lie to them, anyway. In fact, experts know that the way to any woman's heart is first lying to her face while looking her in the eyes. Yet the big questions remain: Why do men get to engage in all of this dandy duplicity? Shouldn't more women take on the role of becoming big, thin liars?

Today's Independent Woman is in need of a coy con of her own. It's time to fetch back the fib, to keep our eyes on the lies! Ladies, start your eyelids!

To get your fix of eye-popping tricks, you're going to have to fork over some serious lettuce. Fashionable femmes know that it takes cents to make sense. Enter a collection of chic products on the market this very spring, compiled with the very eyes of this very writer. Because ladies, when it comes to men...the eye knows.

Norman Orman's Ultra Sheer Eyelid Glaze in Liquid Colourless, $50

Orman's done it again, this time with makeup so sheer that the glazed doughnuts at the office will look more tarted up than you do. Because men can never tell when we're wearing makeup anyway, but other women (like those wenches at the office) always have a way of finding out.

Potbelly Pete's Pot O' Eye Gunk in Beer Barrel Browns, $111.11

Though the price may seem a little steep, the bottom of the barrel this isn't. Potbelly Pete (real name Peter Straylurk) is a godsend when it comes to crafting colours that call out to the modern man. From lagers to porters, the array of eye booze will leave you drunk at first sight. Not recommended for pregnant women.

Leslie Ashley Whitney's Urgent Lust for All Things Pretty, Colourful, and Pleasing to Leslie Ashley Whitney's Eyes $85

Confused critics have been eyeing Leslie Ashley Whitney for several months now, since this past fall's Frantic Fusion fashion show. Little is known about the mysterious Leslie Ashley Whitney, except that he is most likely not a woman, but merely a man with three androgynous names. Yet this is more reason to trust Leslie Ashley Whitney's brand of cosmetics, particularly his scintillating spring line of eye candy ("Go! Find-Leslie-Ashley-Whitney Green" and "Stop! I-See-Leslie-Ashley-Whitney Red" are must have hues!) If the three names don't do it for you, then perhaps the companion CD of spoken word poetry will. The standout track on this album is clearly "Initials in Court", with the lyrics of "I am Leslie Ashley Whitney! I am the LAW!" Fashion police take note, as there is a new sheriff of style this spring.

Whichever of these fine products you purchase this spring, just remember to pile them on proudly. Sheer or bold, there is simply no substitute for the superficial illusion of makeup. Plus, any of these eye colours are delightful for taking away the focus on the watery, red eyes brought on by those pesky springtime allergies. Thus, until womankind has found a way to combat nature, we shall resort to masking its side effects with only the classiest of cosmetics. •*HW*•

Supermodel Moms-to-be

By Sharon Grehan

Egregious: It's amazing, it's sort of like something is growing in you, it's hard to explain. I had a cyst once but it was nothing like this.

My trainer/husband says I've never looked more beautiful, that I'm positively glowing. I know he's lying because he refers to overweight people as fat pigs but I do appreciate his sensitivity. If it's a girl we are going to name her Brian and if it's a boy were going to name him Molly.

Santas: I didn't know I was pregnant until I was five months along, I haven't had a regular period since I was eight so I didn't notice anything for a while, but two months ago I went to the doctor when I felt something moving. We'd had sushi the night before and I was really frightened that the fish wasn't dead when I ate it. You can imagine my relief when I found out it was going to be a baby instead of a tuna.

I have big plans for this baby; I have so much I want to teach it. I can teach it how to swim and tell it all about the two basic food groups. I think it's going to be a riot having someone to hang around with all the time.

Jessica Sang: It's a real spiritual thing, it's like something that is bigger than you, only not really because then you would tip over. I feel in touch with myself and my feelings for the first time since I got on the cover of *Vogue.*

I've been researching Eastern philosophies and religions with a Western influence. I've pretty well designed my own. I want to be everything to this child: mother, preacher, advisor, friend, personal trainer. This child will be a smaller version of me at first and then it will grow larger as time goes by. I put my faith in Buddha and Jesus and Oprah and keep my fingers crossed all day every Tuesday.

Suze: this is my second child so I know what to look forward to. My first child Jejeune has been the light of my life. Whenever I visit her in Switzerland I feel whole. I share her joys and triumphs whenever I get a free moment. I also learned from my mistakes because this time I'm pretty sure who the father is.

It is difficult being a single mother, having to reorganize my life for her yearly visits so this time I've learned to prioritize. I put myself first, and my career second.

Copper: To be honest I thought this would ruin my career but thanks to Cindy motherhood is pretty hot right now, so the timing was good.

I worry about all the normal things, will this child be healthy, smart, pretty, thin? Will I lose the seven pounds I've gained so far? But all those things seem unimportant when I start to look ahead and realize I can have a beer in six months. •*HW*•

Herstory: LTB – One Woman's Triumph Over Adversity

By Sharon Grehan

IT WAS LATE October 1998. Dr. Jane McDonald left the hospital after a long, especially gruelling day and looked forward to a relaxing dinner with her family.

Just an ordinary day. Until something extraordinary happened. Halfway through the meal Jane felt an odd sensation.

"My family was talking to me but I couldn't make out words, only sounds. The room seemed to spin and the sound rose to intolerable levels, before I knew what was happening I was standing at the head of the table screaming 'Shut up, shut up all of you!'"

Jane's breaking point came just as her daughter finished a story about playschool and her husband started to talk about his day as a statistician.

"As much as I hate to say it, I realized that night that my family was the most boring family alive. I couldn't believe it, I fell to pieces. I remember my husband rushed to my side, gave me a Neo-Citron and ushered me off to bed.

"I thought that it was an isolated incident, but it was just the start."

Before long Jane found even the simplest exchanges hard to bear. She was unable to visit her neighbourhood convenience store any longer because of the proprietor's insistence upon talking about the weather and dinner at the in-laws, once tolerable, became an impossibility.

"My mother-in-law is interested in miniatures," Jane says simply.

After a few weeks, Jane found it increasingly difficult to leave the house. She found the only joy she received was in television commercials. She was unable to communicate with her family any longer.

"My husband took me to doctor after doctor. I was diagnosed as having everything from Lyme disease to Yuppie flu. One doctor even suggested that it might be gout."

Frustrated, Jane sunk into a deep depression until her husband found Dr. Harold Reloy or "Dr. Hal" on the Internet.

"It was a last resort; I have to admit I did not have high hopes. His web site had a dancing stethoscope and most of the links were dead, but I was desperate."

The doctor listened to Jane's story and immediately came up with a diagnosis. She was suffering from a Low Threshold of Boredom. (LTB)

"At first I was stunned; you never believe it's going to happen to you. This is the kind of thing that happens to other people. After the diagnosis I went into denial."

Jane closed herself in her room and lost herself in the world of ad imagery. Dancing hot-dogs and talking sodas became her friends. Her husband tried to pretend there was nothing wrong. He hoped Jane would just snap out of it, but as the days spread into weeks he found he could not cope.

As a last desperate measure, he got the family together and they staged an intervention. Jane needed help.

"It was awful," Jane says. "I felt humiliated. I made a deal with them: if they would just shut the hell up I would do anything."

Through Dr. Hal, Michael was able to find a clinic that offered treatment for LTB. The Eaves, once an upper-crust spa, has been transformed into a LTB treatment centre.

"I was very frightened at first, but Dr. Hal put me at ease when he explained to me that LTB wasn't my problem, it was everyone else's problem." Jane admits.

"You see, human beings have lost the ability to edit themselves." Dr. Hal explains "This was perfectly acceptable before we had television, but it is unnatural now. So we like to take a positive interactive prosalve tolerant adaptive co-grain approach."

During family therapy sessions only the LTB patient gets to talk. Dr. Hal has a theory it will help to balance the scale and just might help to cure years of resentment. Then they are given coping methods. When a Terminally Boring (TB) person (anyone who adversely affects an LTB patient) is talking, the LTB-er is instructed to wait ten seconds. If in that ten seconds they find that the TB-ers conversation does not involve them directly, the patients are taught to make a snipping motion with their fingers forcing the TB to become more aware. After the snipping or "cut" motion is mastered then patients move onto the "tiny key lip lock" gesture and when these methods don't work the LTB patient is instructed to say "You don't interest me," explain why, then walk away.

Jane had to summon up her courage to tell her mother-in-law that her Red Rose Tea miniatures were not only uninteresting, they were also ugly and worthless. Next she told her husband that statistics are only interesting if they are made up, but the hardest of all was telling her four year old that while playschool was probably very interesting to her, it was mind numbing to anyone else. No one cared who ate who's lunch, who went poo in the cloakroom, who could fit an entire Lego door in their mouth. And a big by the way —mommy already knows the alphabet.

"It was very painful watching my child cry" Jane chokes back a sob as she recalls the painful experience. "but it is a matter of survival."

"Three out of ten people across the US and Canada suffer from LTB and seven out of ten people are TB." says Michael clasping his wife's hand. "I found this very revealing because when you look at..."

"That does not interest me in the least because your stories are boring," Jane interrupts, smiling warmly at her saviour. •*HW*•

QUIZ: Are You Boring?

By Sharon Grehan

You think "how are you doing?" means "how are you doing?"
When someone else speaks during a conversation it ruins your concentration.
When you are telling a story, you find interruptions along the lines of "you already told me this" rude, but continue on anyway.
You feel if a sentence doesn't start with "I" it isn't worth continuing.
You find a flat, even tone the best one for relaying information.
You end every party with your wedding video.
The bus driver knows all about your divorce six years ago.
If you lose your train of thought you find "ummmmm" or "uhhhhhhhh" valuable placeholders to keep you from losing the floor.
In your mind, listening is a process where you scan phrases for segues.
You feel high school chess club stories have to be told again and again and again. They never lose their richness.
You are completely incapable of hearing anything after you say the phrase "Well, if you want my advice..."
You find other people very boring.

ANSWERS

If you answered yes to three or more questions, then you are boring. Very, very boring. *Trés TB!* We'd try to help you but you'd probably just tell us things.
If you skipped the quiz and went right to the answers then you could be suffering from LTB. Go back to the article and have a friend read it to you in a funny voice or act it out with sock puppets. If it still doesn't hold you, you may wish to contact Dr. Hal. •*HW*•

Join the Fatkins Revolution!

By Elizabeth Hanes

ARE YOU SICK of knowing no one who sees you in a backless dress will ever be able to count your vertebrae? Disgusted that no one ever says to you, "You're so thin! Are you ill?" Morose because you know whenever you wave goodbye to loved ones, your upper arms are going to flap like bedsheets on a clothesline?

You're not alone. Research indicates that 99% of women have given up on calorie counting. But it doesn't have to be this way. Just because you've given up on weight LOSS doesn't mean you have to give up on weight GAIN.

The Fatkins Diet eliminates the unwanted side effects of dieting: cravings, hunger, and weight loss. Designed for the woman who's made a conscious decision to let herself go, this carefully structured eating plan will help you feel full from sunrise to sunset, while at the same time reducing your energy level to near zero. No longer will you feel the urge to exert yourself through tasks like vacuuming or bathing. Instead, you can lie around all day, watching re-runs of *Angela: The Baby Who Shouldn't Have Been Born But Was and How She Overcame All Odds to Become Queen of the Pygmies* on the Lifetime Network for Women.

Phase One: Induction

The name "induction" signifies that the purpose of this phase is to induce your body to shift from being shaped like an unlit taper to a fully melted pillar candle. During induction, you'll change your body's chemistry to achieve "cellulitis" and "osmosis." "Cellulitis" prepares your cells to accept more fat than they ever thought they could hold. "Osmosis" is the process by which the body adds fat via the ocular nerve.

Induction is designed to do all of the following for you:

- Efficiently switch your body from an efficient carbohydrate-burning metabolism to a fat-storing machine.
- De-stabilize your blood sugar levels in order to bring you a variety of useful and fun symptoms, such as mood swings (useful for keeping children away from your bag of Cheetos) and lightheadedness (a fun way to experience the intoxicating effects of liquor without the expense of actually buying any).
- Curb your cravings by giving in to them.
- Encourage your body to develop addictions to sugar, fats, caffeine and calories.

During induction, you'll get all of your nutrition from high-calorie junk foods, such as potato chips, deep fried Snickers bars, non-diet colas, cheese-covered cheese tortellini in cheese sauce, and Lucky Charms. You'll soon learn what a misnomer "empty calories" is.

Unfortunately, the induction phase is not how you will eat for the rest of your life. This part of the diet only lasts two weeks. Enjoy it while you can.

Phase Two: Putting On Weight

Congratulations on making it through the induction phase! Not everyone accomplishes this difficult step. At least, not everyone accomplishes it without developing a fatal embolism.

As you move from phase one to phase two, you will tailor the Fatkins Nutritional Approach to your unique tastes. The POW phase is similar to induction in that you'll continue to get most of your nutrition from fats, but you'll also begin incorporating more variety into your menu. You'll add more portions of cookies and candy bars, and most people will also be able to gradually add non-fried meats, non-Wonder bread, and even the occasional vegetable.

Remember, however, that when you move away from the rigid structure of induction into the POW phase, you're re-entering the world of "real" food, where you must make sensible choices to avoid slipping back into an eating pattern that leads to weight loss. You must fight the temptation to indulge in things like apples and broccoli. Yogurt should be avoided at all cost.

Phase Three: Lifetime Maintenance

Hedonism. When it comes to eating, that word sums up the Fatkins approach. You have a right to be as fat as you want to be. And so, this phase is all about feeling satisfied.

At some point, a well-meaning—if fanatical—friend is going to tell you the key to dieting is counting calories, counting carbs, or counting fat grams. That's way too much math! Let's set the record straight so you can deal with these diet infidels and convert them to the Fatkins way.

The most noticeable difference between the Fatkins Nutritional Approach and other eating plans is simple: hunger. The "counting" plans always add up to one thing—acute starvation. On the Fatkins Diet, you eat whatever you want, whenever you want it. This eliminates the number one reason most diets fail: hunger.

Another problem with the "counting" diets? They cause you to lose weight! When a person loses weight, they begin to suffer serious side effects, like energy. The Fatkins plan, on the other hand, induces indolence. Not only can this lead to some pretty rewarding results, such as the kids' being forced to wash their own dishes, but if you're among the very fortunate, you might even make it into the Guinness Book as the "world's fattest woman."

The Diet for the Rest of Us

You know you don't care about being thin anymore. Heck, these days you barely care whether that was mouthwash you gargled with, or yesterday's coffee. You hate your job, you're exhausted, and at this point you'd exchange your firstborn child for a bag of Lay's potato chips and a Barcalounger.

It's time. Join the Fatkins Revolution. •*HW*•

Identity Theft

By Elaine Langlois

IDENTITY THEFT is *the* fashion crime of the 21st century. Before you know it, someone will be stealing your identity and walking around in your Manolo Blahnik pumps.

You are in a particularly dangerous position because there are people all over the North American continent who want to be like you. And why wouldn't they?

How do you know if your identity has been stolen?

Perhaps you come back to your house and find someone else who looks just like you. She is chopping things in your Cuisinart and French-kissing your husband.

Or you might start to feel funny, as if you are coming down with a cold. You find yourself doing things you've never done before, like giving money to the poor, or picking up a book and reading it. You may notice physical changes, such as a difference in the way you walk.

Don't panic.

Call your nearest government agency. See if it has the new gait analysis software the U.S. government is investing in for profiling terrorists. You might also ask the agents to check your irises and facial grooves.

For early detection, your best bet is the Identity Theft Monitoring Kit™ from Sharper Edge. It mounts to any wall and is powered by two C-cell batteries.

What happens when your identity is stolen?

Often, the first sign is unusual charges on your credit card bill, like trips to Mars. Most people don't catch this, however, because they never look at their credit card bills. They just make the minimum payment and go their merry way.

If someone gets your driver's license, they could drive your car. They could go to the ice cream shop and order a double chocolate malted, which would absolutely wreck your diet. They might eat bananas in your car and leave the peels under the seat. They could change all the buttons on the radio and mess with the cupholders.

An identity thief might open a chequing account in your name and write bad cheques. Very bad cheques. Cheques to environmental groups and orphanages. Cheques to pudding fests. We just can't let this sort of thing happen!

How can you prevent identity theft?

The U.S. government provides a set of useful guidelines for guarding against identity theft. You can remember them from this simple acronym: BPGMOK.

BPGMOK. It's sort of like saying *big mop* after a lengthy session with your dentist. BPGMOK. It doesn't matter what the letters stand for, just so long as you remember them.

Don't tell anyone your birthday.

Not just the year, but the exact date as well. In fact, you should probably have several birthday parties for yourself scattered over the year. That way you will get more presents!

Cut down the number of credit cards you carry with you to eight or ten.

What else can you do to prevent identity theft? Don't take anything with you when you go anywhere. Better yet, don't go anywhere. Stay home. Wear a wig. And a mustache. And your housecleaner's clothes. Try speaking in a foreign accent.

How do identity thieves steal your identity?

It used to be that they shoved you into a phone booth, snatched your identity, and sped away. But there aren't that many phone booths anymore, what with everybody talking on cells, so they've had to change their tactics.

Now they come to your house, at night, mostly, when everyone is asleep. They go dumpster-diving through your trash; they slip through broken windowpanes and holes the squirrels have gnawed in the attic. They make off with your Starbucks receipts, your tooth whitener, your knockoff designer fragrances, your highlighted collection of *Cosmopolitans*-anything they can use to counterfeit your identity.

If you've been a victim of identity theft, what should you do?

You probably need to transmogrify

yourself into someone else. Try to pick someone with more money, a better figure, and lots of clothes.

Better yet, what you need is a *secret identity*. One that nobody knows, not even you. You will also need a secret headquarters (maybe have a decorator come in and redo the laundry room), a cape and mask, a decoder ring, and a batpole.

Identity theft can be very traumatic. But you have the power to turn it into a life-affirming experience. Think of it as an opportunity to rediscover yourself. To proclaim your identity to the world. To purchase every monogrammed product you can lay your hands on.

What's it like, getting your identity back?

It's painful. It has to be sewn on, like Peter Pan's shadow, and believe me, he was being brave when he clenched his teeth and didn't say it hurt. •*HW*•

HW DISPATCH:

New Line of Cheap Mother's Day Cards for Mediocre Mothers

HALLMARK, RESPONDING TO consumer backlash over the price of Mother's Day greeting cards, has announced a new line aimed at capturing the mediocre mom market. Dubbed "So-So Sentiments," the line will provide value-priced cards for less-than-perfect mothers. With verses such as, "You didn't screw me up as much as you could have / And for that I'm grateful / So I guess you're worth this $1 card," and "I love you / But not as much / As I might / If you weren't / Constantly belittling me," the cards will be priced between 50-cents and $1.50. "We felt there was a real market for cards targeting women who might not otherwise receive a Mother's Day card," said Hallmark spokeswoman Betty Eldridge. "This way, even shoddy mothers – the ones who perhaps don't deserve a flowery $4 sentiment - can be acknowledged as at least adequate" —*E. Hanes*

Drug Czar Announces Tupperware Added to Controlled Substance List

Citing his wife's addiction as a prime example, Drug Czar Enrique Vasquez Smith, announced today that he has unilaterally declared Tupperware a controlled substance. "My whole house has been taken over by the colourful plastic bowls with airtight lids," he said in a prepared statement. "My wife began by purchasing 'harmless' Rubbermaid products, then moved up to Tupperware. Now, she can't get enough of the stuff. To make matters worse, she regularly has her dealer come to the house, where the two of them recruit others to the deadly addiction." Under the new law, anyone caught possessing more than 3 pieces of Tupperware will be subject to federal criminal charges with sentences ranging from fines to life in prison. —*E. Hanes*

The Rules of Family: Advice from Donna Corleone

By Pamela Monk

DEAR MADRONE:

I am most confused. My wife, who is a doormat, has a mother who is a big problem. Not to me, my mother in law loves me, this I don't understand, for I would like nothing better than to see her, well if not wearing cement overshoes, with a few pebbles in her pockets, if you get my drift.

What the deal is, I finally couldn't stand how she runs my Cecilia to the ground, all the time, no matter what Cecilia does, it's not good enough. I told her off, politely, of course, in a very thoughtful well composed letter, four pages, which I sent without telling Ceil. Now the mother calls to say that from now on we are both dead to her. Ceil is corked off at me. Is this fair?

Sign me,
I just love my wife, what did I do that's so wrong?
Mahwah.

Dear Wrong,

There are times when I could just weep from the basic stupidity of *jamokes* like you. Do you not read my columns?? Do you not understand that if you were to throw out every other rule of family and only followed this one, your life would be 3000 per cent better than the living hell you have created for yourself? Why do I bother to breathe??

There is only one solution to your problem. Go to your mother-in-law, throw yourself at her feet, and grovel like a whipped dog, and beg her forgiveness.

And that may not be enough. You must also go to your wife, and declare that you were taken with the fever and had no idea you had committed such a terrible act, and swear upon your own mother's head that you will never do any such thing ever again. Perhaps then, and then only, you can begin to repair the damage you have caused. Jewelry to both women could not hurt, but remember never pearls.

God bless,
Donna

Dear Readers-

The above letter is so aggravating, what *agita!* I feel I must make a special plea to you, yes you, look at me when I'm talking to you. Even though I give good advice, the best, it is clear that some of you are determined to ignore what you know is right. Now I say if you're going to make a mess of things, which sometimes cannot be helped, I realize that, please do it deliberately, not like this idiot who thinks he is making things better by going behind his wife's back to insult her mother. This is not smart.

Never get in between someone and their mother. NEVER. I don't care if said mother is the burr on the *coulie* of the person who is near and dear to you. I don't care if 110% of the time said near and dear complains and weeps over the injustices and cruelties perpetrated. I don't care if the mother makes John Gotti look like Our Lady Of Fatima. There are only two things you have the right to say on this matter.

One: I love your mother, but then other people's mothers are always charming.

Two: Your mother can't be all bad, after all she raised you and you are wonderful.

That's it. Nothing else is safe. If you choose to go another route, which you may feel to be necessary for the health and or sanity of your loved one, then be prepared to reap the whirlwind. People do not thank you when you kick them in the teeth.

God bless, Donna

Chapter Six – June

Get in Shape with Ballroom Dancing
By Mike Boone

THERE ARE MANY accepted ways to work up a sweat but there's only one that allows you to do it while wearing high heels. Ballroom dancing takes many forms and therefore it is easy to accomplish an entire workout by utilizing only a few of the most basic steps.

The Waltz

This is one of the all-time great warm up routines. By doing the box step, you will be up and tripping the light fantastic after only one easy lesson.

The gentleman steps forward with the left foot then asks the lady for a dance. She turns slightly and answers, "No!" He shifts his weight; steps back with his right foot and closes his feet to the starting position as he makes his way back to the stag line. He sits down and tries to look cool. This part alone can induce a participant to easily sweat off four or five pounds.

The lady will do the same thing except she begins with the second step and winks at the bartender who just happens to look exactly like Mel Gibson.

If you are a heavyweight you can still be light on your feet. Only be sure to use extra caution so as not to topple over during all the weight shifting. As a heavy couple it will be your responsibility to try alternating your feet to avoid becoming entangled with one another thus reducing the risk of injury to other dancers should you fall in tandem.

Overall, this is a pretty safe dance step for a couple of reasons. First, the box step was designed in such a way that you never really move from the exact spot you began from. Secondly, the only time the waltz is actually performed nowadays is when the father of the bride dances with his daughter at her wedding reception. (If she remembered to invite him, that is.) That's only provided someone shows up with an accordion, as the only available prerecorded waltzes can be found on rare turn of the century vitrollas written by and for dead people.

The Swing

Now that you're warmed up you are ready to move on to a medium/fast tempo. The swing requires additional coordination as it incorporates slow steps, quick steps, rock steps and solo movements by the lady. Finding a partner who can excel at the solo movements holds the key to distinguishing one's self while performing this dance – particularly if you happen to suck at the slow steps, quick steps and rock steps.

The swing gets its name from the fact that the gentleman swings his partner by whirling her under his arm. You signal when you are about to execute a turn by gently raising your left arm on the first slow step and shouting, "Here we go!" Follow through on the turn by pushing the lady through with your right hand giving both of you an opportunity to resynchronize your steps. Failure to readjust timing risks accidentally pushing on your partner's breast where you could find yourself bunny hopping on your head right out the front door.

The Cha Cha

As its name implies, this one is a very complex, high-energy dance step employing advanced footwork. Start with our left foot forward and transfer your weight back onto the right foot. (This is where the real fun comes in.) Take three small steps to the left and say, "Cha, cha, cha." (Fun, right?) Now do the entire thing in reverse, starting with your right foot and ending with a backwards "Cha, cha, cha." Don't ask me why, just do it.

The Cha Cha can be particularly challenging, as you will most likely be the only couple on the dance floor with guts enough to try it—notably if you happen to be in a cowboy bar at the time and especially if it has no dance floor (or music).

In cases like this you might get away with it if instead of, "Cha, cha, cha," you said, "Achy breaky" or something like that. However, I doubt it. Even if you tried wearing cowboy boots and a ten-gallon hat, line dancing rarely requires a backwards arabesque. Alternatively, maybe they do. I don't know.

Maybe you should just order a sarsaparilla and leave quietly before somebody hits you.

Turkey Shuffle

All forms of ballroom dancing require the participants to maintain a very stiff, rigid spine. If done correctly it should look as if you desperately need to go to the bathroom and each movement is producing unspeakable agony in your kidneys.

The only exception to this I can think of is Slam Dancing but I consider Slam Dancing undignified so we'll stick with something more regal like the Funky Monkey. It looks nothing like the name suggests. Oh, sure, the gentleman slings the lady over his shoulder and jumps up and down making "Eeek!" noises but he does it all in a very majestic manner.

The footwork is a series of improvised stomps and kicks. When done correctly, hand movements are meant to enhance the overall aristocratic appearance of the dance. These can take the form of scratching your bum, slapping yourself on the side of the head or pounding on your bared chest - and the gentleman's steps are equally as colourful.

You might want to try a charming American version of this dance step called "The Flaming Leap of Death." Shifting your weight onto your right foot, jump up onto a table and begin swinging from the chandelier as the maitre d' pokes at you with blazing hot shish kebab skewers. This fanciful variation is made even more dramatic if the lady jumps onto the headwaiter's back while keeping to the rhythm of the marimba.

This step gives you a pretty decent workout and now you should be thinking about a good, cool down routine.

The Fox Trot

This popular cool down is done in four-four time. Set your metronome to *largo,* between forty and sixty. Trying to look your most elegant, clasp hands, taking care to have the thumbs meet at eye level with the woman's gaze. This enables her to wipe sweat from her nose without drawing undue attention to her nostrils.

After a few choruses of *Mame* your upper limbs will begin to twitch as the tendons in your forearms calcify. Three minutes in this position is the equivalent of bench-pressing eight hundred pounds.

Even middle-aged debutantes are considered quite formidable arm wrestlers midway through the cotillion season. If you work at it, you too could have the arms of an aging marmoset.

Turn off the music and return to your seats. Lovely job, well done. •*HW*•

Fitness Secrets of the Superstars

By Elizabeth Hanes

IT'S SUMMER AND once again you've made "dieting" or "getting in shape" your top priority even though we both know you'll be crossing that one off the list the first time you pass a KFC.

For shame! Why is it that YOU always fail at dieting, yet even B-list celebrities like Shakira seem to have no problem maintaining their goal weight?

We have the answers! Simply follow these fitness secrets of the superstars, and you'll be on your way to Thin City in no time.

Katie Couric

The perky hostess of NBC's *Today Show* is a source of seemingly boundless energy. We wondered how she did it.

"I'm naturally peppy," she told us as she drank her eighth double-espresso shot at a little café in Manhattan, "Peppy, peppy, peppy." Grinning widely, she explained, "I find I need v-v-very little sleep. I can get by on, oh, 30 to 45 minutes a day. 30 to 45 minutes a day. That really frees up time for other activities. Other stuff. Like dieting and exercising."

The daytime diva dropped to the floor of the coffee shop and did a quick 25 push-ups, much to the surprise of our reporter and the diners at the lunch counter. Springing to her feet, Katie said, "I do that several times a day to relieve stress and build upper arm strength, in case I have to reach over and smack Matt Lauer during taping. Not on the air, of course."

"When it comes to diet, I stick to raw foods and coffee. For breakfast, I often enjoy an orange, unpeeled, with five or six pots of the studio's coffee, and lunch might be a large head of cauliflower washed down with a shot of espresso and fourteen cups of 100% Columbian coffee. I don't usually eat dinner because I'm just not that hungry."

Katie then turned and bellowed, "More espresso, dammit!" at the counterman before sprinting out the door, presumably to jog the 27 blocks to Rockefeller Center for her next taping.

Catherine Zeta Jones

"Staying fit is a real issue for me," Catherine told us. "I mean, most days I can't even walk at a good clip when I'm shopping because I have to wait for Michael, doddering along behind me. And making love ten or twelve times a day doesn't burn nearly as many calories as he said it would."

So how does the beautiful movie star keep her gorgeous figure?

"I'm not shy about eating," she asserts. "I mean, every morning I get up and have a Cheerio, a couple cups of coffee; I might even look at a piece of toast. After that, I spend two hours exercising. Sometimes I briskly walk from one end of the mansion to another, or I might brush my long, thick black hair, which really tones my upper arms. And several times a day, I make it a point to bend down and pick up one of my children instead of having the nanny hand it to me. That helps me keep a trim waistline."

Jennifer Lopez

The pop princess turned movie starlet has every reason to stay in shape these days, what with a hot movie career and her marriage to Marc Anthony. Being so busy, how does she possibly find time to exercise? We caught up with Jennifer at a video shoot in L.A. recently.

"I'm so in love right now, it's pretty easy to stay motivated not to overeat," Jenny told us while eyeing a handsome electrician on the set. "I love to cook, which is nice because I can control the quality of what I put in my mouth." She winked at an assistant director and licked her lips. "It's important to me that food is tasty while being as low-fat as possible," she said, pausing a moment to rub herself up and down against a makeup artist re-powdering her for the next scene.

"Marc and I like to exercise together," she explained, blowing kisses at a muscular dancer on the other side of the set and silently mouthing what appeared to be the words "later, later" until he nodded and slipped away. "We practice yoga every day because it helps us focus our energy forces and meld them into one. Together, we're unstoppable," she smiled, leaning across to tongue-kiss us. "When you have found your life partner, it's so much easier to stay in control. I think that's the key."

That's all there is to it, ladies! Remember: if they can do it, so can you. •*HW*•

To Breed or Not to Breed

By Jessica Becht

SO YOUR MARRIAGE is falling apart?

Only a few years ago, swathed in polyester tulle, tipsy from the domestic "champagne," you were led by your new husband in your first dance as man and wife. Leering at you in his endearing way, he trod gently on your toes. Your eyes were full of hope and starlight.

Yet now that divorce lawyer with the flashy picture on the back of the phone book beckons to you in dreams. You are on your hands and knees, once again making room for your suitcase, as you scare up a retainer fee from the spare change on the floor of your sister's closet. Where did it all go wrong?

You know you'll never really go through with the divorce. Neither one of you can pay the mounting Visa bills on your own. So why not act to hold your marriage together? The time-honoured method of doing so is having a baby.

"A baby?" you gasp, aghast. "Why would I want to trade my almost bikini-perfect form for monstrous rotundity?" As a jaded modern woman, you cannot perceive the advantages of creating an autonomous creature that will be able to state, "I hate you, Mommy," with faultless diction before you've even lost the baby weight.

But have you considered how much your husband longs to impregnate you? He may seem indifferent, but with you knocked up, he'd finally feel like a real man. Swelling machismo can only benefit your faltering love life. No one wants to pay child support on a paltry salary like his. That's right, a baby is the glue that holds a crumbling marriage together.

Conventional wisdom states that raising children is difficult, expensive, and time-consuming. False. Children can be taught to perform household chores as soon as they are able to walk unaided. Even a two-year old can recycle beer cans or empty ashtrays. In some countries with forward thinking labour laws, a child can augment the household income with a lucrative factory job. Why not move to one of them? Arguments with your husband are sure to decrease once your house is sparkly clean and you have a third income to help with the never-ending debt spiral.

There are also social benefits to having well-trained children. For example, as a respectable adult you cannot point to overweight or unattractive strangers in public and make loud, hurtful comments. This is considered rude. Yet, your darling four-year-old daughter will be able to. When, clad in a ruffled pink dress (that one she made herself in a Malaysian sweatshop), she exclaims with innocent wonder, "Mommy, why is that fat lady over there buying so many boxes of cookies?" you might chuckle indulgently before replying in a stage whisper, "Now, now, it isn't nice to say such things. You don't want the fat lady over there to feel bad about her very serious eating disorder and the fact that she disgusts normal people with her presence." Free to fling gratuitous insults at strangers, your self-esteem will soar. Your husband is sure to consider your newfound confidence attractive and dump that stripper he's been hanging around with.

It is time to dispel your final objection to motherhood. All the cosmetic surgery you've invested in has unfortunately not enhanced your genetic code. A child that resembles your unaltered self might be embarrassing. Don't worry! Simply solicit a "college fund" from prospective grandparents. Dip into these accounts whenever your child enters an awkward stage. Why would your child need to go to college anyway? Formal education won't be necessary with all the work experience your offspring is sure to have.

To breed or not to breed? That is the question this article has just answered for you. Get up off the closet floor, and go spend the spare change you've just gathered on a Frederick's of Hollywood teddy. Your husband is going to need something stimulating. •*HW*•

Health Alert: Hidden Household Hazards

By SB Shoemaker

ON THE DAY THAT Myrtle Marquart became a statistic, she never knew what hit her. That fateful morning, her vacuum cleaner malfunctioned, racing out of control when the speed governor failed. If she had reacted differently, Myrtle might have survived, but she failed to let go as the machine quickly accelerated to speeds in excess of 80 miles per hour. By then, it was too late.

Myrtle had become another casualty of an unreported epidemic raging across the country. According to records kept for no particular reason by an obscure government agency, housework kills.

Women are three times more likely to die in hideous tragedies involving turkey-basters than they are from car accidents, falls, bee stings, squirrel attacks and freak electrocutions combined. Statistics for men, who typically have little or no experience with housework, are not available.

All types of housework, not just those involving appliances, can be hazardous. Esther Bogges was found on the floor of her living room by her husband, the apparent victim of an out-of-control feather duster. She has no memory of the attack. Police investigators believe that Mrs. Bogges may have grasped the duster by the feather end and, instead of dusting, accidentally beat herself unconscious with the handle. The duster remains in custody.

Betty Lou Carbuncle is still recovering from her encounter with a runaway eggbeater. "Once it got going, I just couldn't stop it," she recalls. As she started to spin the beater, "it took on a life of its own, like it was possessed." She used one hand to call her pastor, but that only made the situation worse. "When I tried to seek the Lord's help, it just went insane."

Mrs. Carbuncle fought for her life as the eggbeater savagely splattered her walls and ceiling with cornbread batter. She gives full credit for her salvation to a higher power. She grabbed her Bible and jammed it into the beaters, disabling them long enough for her to escape without permanent injury.

These women are not alone. Every year, millions of lives are senselessly lost in accidents just like these. Most people are simply unaware of how dangerous their homes can be. Just ask former beauty salon owner Candy Demarco. "I never thought my dryer could do a thing like that. I knew it ate socks, and sometimes shredded delicates, but I never suspected how vicious it could be."

When she removed Mr. Whiskers, her prize-winning Persian cat, from the dryer at the end of the air fluff cycle, the static buildup discharged, igniting the fumes from her Basement Boutique Nail Emporium. The resulting fireball incinerated the room immediately overhead along with everything in it, including the members of the Red Hat Bridge Club who had just dealt their last hand.

In response to reports of the growing threat, the Director of the U.S. Department of Homeland Security hired an undocumented maid before releasing a statement that insists people are secure in their own homes and the danger is "overrated."

Until the government decides to act, prevention is the key to personal safety. If at all possible, avoid doing housework entirely. If some housework becomes essential, try to find someone else to do it for you, preferably someone you don't like very much, or ask your husband, or children. If that isn't convenient, use the buddy system, as some appliances may be intimidated if outnumbered.

Whatever you do, remember to stay calm if you find yourself in a threatening situation. Gloria Bosanova discovered this the hard way. "I was minding my own business, cleaning the toilet, when the lid suddenly dropped on my head. The pressure was incredible, like being crushed in the jaws of a great white shark. I almost passed out. Luckily I didn't panic, but if I hadn't had my cell phone with me, I don't know what would have happened." •*HW*•

"Every year, millions of lives are senselessly lost in accidents just like these."

What Your Eyebrows Say About You

By Sharon Grehan

IF THE EYES ARE the window to the soul, then the eyebrows must be the window treatment. Find out what they say about you!

The Untamed

Your brows say "Look at me, I gave up a long time ago!" Your favourite colour is beige and you talk behind everyone's back. You have a secret talent for decoupage and have a ham and cheese sandwich rotting in your filing cabinet.

You will never marry and you will be referred to in later years as "that spooky woman with all the cats."

The Curve

Lovable, cute, dimwitted with no sense of humour. You secretly hate your best friend and love true crime novels. Your favourite colour is eggplant and you chose a Pekinese because it set off your skin tone. You think wrestling is real and the ozone layer is not.

You will marry twice and become a barfly when you are fifty-two.

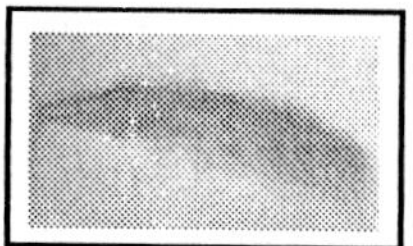

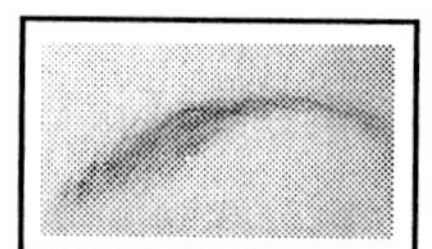

The Arch

Wise, witty and a tad arrogant. Your favourite colour is teal blue and you keep your diary under a cashmere sweater in the third drawer to the right in your dresser. You are fond of animals but unable to keep one because of your nail polish remover addiction.

You only read book-liners and you are frightened of whisk brooms.

You will have three children with three different husbands and become famous as a result of a cosmetic surgery screw-up.

The Straight Arrow

Everyone comes to you for advice but they never take it because they think you are stupid. You steal Post-it notes from work and have a crush on your mailman. You love reading and fancy yourself a poet. People rarely remember your name and you are generally referred to as that "sneaky" girl.

Your favourite colour is mustard and your dry-cleaning ticket is in your windbreaker.

You will inherit money when you are forty-two and blow it all in a ballroom dance

Ladies' Guide to Lawn Care

By Elaine Langlois

THE FIRST STEP in lawn care is simple: *get someone else to do it.* Preferably some muscular fellow named Rolando or Sven. Sitting shirtless athwart a riding mower making crop circles in your lawn while you laze in the house, sipping a latté and enjoying the view. Mmm!

If Step 1 is not within the realm of financial possibility, don't despair. Lawn care is in fact the perfect hobby for the discriminating woman, as much of it consists of ruthlessly taking out what *doesn't belong* and putting mulch around everything that looks just right.

Mulch is delivered to your driveway in a mountain level with your second-story windows and is transported in dribs and drabs, via Little Tikes wagon, to the appropriate spots. One load will last you all season, because it will take you that long to get it off the driveway to wherever you want it.

What should I wear to do yard work?

Since the 1950s, when women who stayed at home began spending part of the day outside doing yard work instead of all day inside doing housework, a dress, stockings (later to give way to pantyhose), pearls, and high heels have been preferred for tasks such as trimming the rosebushes and putting up storm shutters. An alternative for today's women: Capri pants, a ruffled tank, and slingbacks. As long as you're going to be out there, you might as well do a little advertising.

What tools should I use?

If this were the "Gentlemen's Guide to Lawn Care," the answer of course would be power tools. Men must have power. They would not be caught dead raking but must have at least a leaf blower and a chipper-shredder to see them through the autumn. If a man sees a wistful, lonely dandelion sitting along the fence, he gets a weed whacker and levels everything within 40 meters. If your significant other is such a fellow, I refer you to the bestseller *Men Who Use Power Tools and the Women Who Love Them.*

Women are more low-tech, thrifty, and minimalistic. Like my aunt, who can clean her entire kitchen with one paper towel. Ladies' tools for yard work: grass shears, pruning shears, little clippers, broom, dustpan, dandelion fork, scuffle hoe, rake, gloves.

What about poison ivy?

A common problem in even the best yards, poison ivy causes an irritating rash for those unfortunate enough to be allergic to it.

Naturalists say we can recognize poison ivy by its three leaves and red stem. This simple statement encapsulates the whole problem with nature: *everything has three leaves and a red stem.* Get out in your yard and you will see what I mean.

Your best approach is probably to torch the whole thing and put down artificial turf. On the other hand, a poison ivy groundcover is a good way of discouraging pesky neighbourhood children from playing in your yard.

Now a few words about what's hot and what's not in lawns and yards this year:

What's Hot

Conformity. This is the first word in lawn care. Witness the growth, in many better neighbourhoods, of lawn care police, armed with rulers for checking the length of your grass, anonymous complaints from neighbours about the state of your shrubbery, and lists of plantings both approved and banned: *"You! Over there! Put down the inexpensive native plant and back away slowly."*

Grass must be ethnically pure. Woe betide the lawn that harbours violets or clover. If yours does, rigorously apply a chemical fertilizer. Your backyard pond may sport a variety of deformed frogs, and your organic radicchio may look like something spawned near a nuclear power plant, but your lawn will be uniform and pristine.

Mole traps. Goodness forbid that some hapless creature out of *The Wind in the Willows* should make ridges and mounds of dirt in your lawn in the process of trying to exist. Traps that skewer the mole so it dies in agony (but underground, so as to spare you any unpleasantness) are quite in vogue. The plunger conveniently detaches so you can cook up your kill on the Weber. Try it with a little strawberry-mango curry sauce!

"Lawn care is in fact the perfect hobby for the discriminating woman..."

Dogs. Just as every dog must have its day, every yard must have its golden retriever or lab. Purebred dogs are hot, but fences tall enough to keep them in the yard are not. Unlike the friendly mutts of our youth, dogs these days seem incapable of distinguishing attack-wise, between an armed felon and a neighbour who has passed the house nearly every day for the past five years. Hence the tender disciplines of electronic fencing.

Water features. Ponds, waterfalls, and fountains are in, way in. Also outdoor showers ($3,000-$7,500). Risks of malaria and West Nile virus are greatly exaggerated.

Walls. No neighbourhood of McMansions is complete without a wall clearly distinguishing those who live *within* from those who live *without.*

Feeders. Feeding birds is perennially hot. Feeding squirrels (affectionately referred to by some as tree rats) is not. If a "No Squirrels" sign doesn't help, put up one of those expensive, complicated baffle feeders designed in competitions by engineering students. Know, however, that it will not work for long. The feeder has not been designed that squirrels cannot penetrate, particularly the ones with slide rules and pencils behind their ears. It is worth noting that the same people who create these devices that cannot outwit rodents go on to design the bridges and other structures we use every day.

What's Not

Annuals. Annuals are beautiful and cheap and look great in your yard. So you buy a few flats. But then you must put them in. That's perhaps 160 plants you'll be digging holes for in the next 24 to 48 hours. Escaping prisoners dig less.

Annuals require more care than infants. For one thing, they can get mold. For another, they have the annoying habit of dying if not watered daily. And of course, they kick off at the first cold snap, so next year you will have to fork out more money and repeat the process.

Geese. Lawn geese are out. The new statuary that you must purchase and dress for various personal and weather events and seasons depends on where you live. Many places have their symbolic animals. In Canada, it's the beaver. In Cincinnati, the pig. In Massachusetts, the cod. In Washington, D.C., the weasel.

Gnomes. Despite their cameo roles in *Amelie* and the second and fourth Harry Potter books, gnomes have not made a comeback.

Where are we at the end of all this, ladies? With a perfectly manicured lawn that no one does anything on. It looks like nobody lives at your house but that person has very good taste. •*HW*•

Libby Interviews Psychic James Van Praagh

by Sharon Grehan

Dear Readers: Well I'm back from my little break at the clin-, er, spa. I was delighted to find that I would be interviewing James Van Praagh. To be honest as a hard-hitting journalist I was skeptical but after a display of his amazing skill he made a believer out of me!

Libby: Do you want me to dim the lights?

James: No, that's not necessary.

Libby: Maybe light a few candles? Some incense? Spooky music?

James: No, let's get right to it. I'm seeing something. Yes. I'm seeing a woman, definitely a woman. I sense she is a relative – do you know who this is?

Libby: Well like I told you a few minutes ago, my grandmother Lillian passed over years ago in a Woolco. She had a massive heart attack while wrestling over a Butterfly Meadow quilt at a white sale. I honestly suspect it was murder because it was 75% off and...

James: I'm seeing an L...yes it's definitely an "L" and I'm seeing crowds, does that make sense? feeling a pain in my chest, yes definitely my chest. I'm seeing a ring, does that make sense?

Libby: Yes! Yes! She wore a wedding ring!

James: I'm seeing the ring, seeing the ring, it's round and gold, do you understand?

Libby: Yes, that's it! That's her ring! It was silver but she definitely had a ring, it had their initials on the inside...

James: OK. Yes, silver. Silver and round,

I'm seeing letters...
Libby: Yes it was engraved! LK to WK...
James: I'm seeing a man, yes definitely a man...wait, Waldo, Winston, Wolfgang, Wheeler, Wilfred, Wendell, Wesley, Whitney, Wuzzy, Weenie, Wallace, Wayne, Ward, Wilbur, Walter, William...
Libby: William! that was my grandpa's name! This is incredible! I'm feeling the hair on the back of my neck crawl!
James: I'm feeling a pain, I'm getting the impression, yes an impression of chest pain. Did your grandfather have problems with his heart?
Libby: Well, yes, when it stopped. But before that, no.
James: Did he have a problem with his lungs?
Libby: No.
James: I'm feeling pain in the head did he have trouble with his head please? Neck region? Top of his legs or arms? Feet? Maybe upper to lower back?
Libby: Yes! He had a bad back!
James: Yes, I'm feeling back pain. I'm seeing a photo of this man, do you understand?
Libby: I have a photo of him! How could you have known that? Oh, gosh I'm shaking – do they have any advice for me?
James: Your grandmother loves you...
Libby: Really?
James: She wants you to be careful, don't smoke in gas stations, don't use the blow dryer in the bathtub, don't operate heavy machinery while drunk.
Libby: Oh my God, Nonnie? Nonnie I've always wanted to ask you, do you know where your good silver went? We tore the floorboards apart looking for it but nothing.
James: I'm sensing the initial "J."
Libby: I have the feeling my sister Blanche who is a greedy no-goodnik might have taken the silver, but so far it's just a suspicion.
James: John, Joe, Johnny, Jeffrey, Jeremiah, Joseph, Jinx, James, Jim, Jimmy J...who is this please?
Libby: Even if she could give me a hint, because that silver is worth thousands now.
James: Jacob, Jacqueline, Julian, Jefferson, Jed, Jim, Jane, Josh, Judy, Jeremiah, Jennifer, Jasper, Jean, Jamie, Jarvis, Jason, Joanne, Jo-Jo, Jack, Jill...
Libby: No, don't know anyone with J...
James: Or K, I'm definitely seeing the initial K; do you know a person with the initial K, who is this please?
Libby: Let me think...
James: Kilroy, Kevin, Kieran, Kathy, Ken, Kenneth, Karen...
Libby: Wait! A Karen used to live next door to me in my old neighbourhood!
James: Karen, that's it. Karen, definitely Karen. She is showing me something, what is this please?
Libby: Oooooo, I don't know. Why would Karen want to talk to me? The only time we spoke was when I threatened to sue her for cutting down my maple. Beautiful tree kept the sun from burning out my retinas, but no, she worshipped the sun and took

down that beautiful tree. She had a face that looked like a baseball mitt probably because of all of the UV...

James: I'm getting the sense that she forgives you.

Libby: Forgives me? For what? I didn't cut down *her* tree, why don't you tell her for me, that I hope the Garden of Paradise still looks nice after she gets her paws on the pruning shears. Also you can tell her...wait a minute, she's not dead.

James: ...Yes, that's what she wants to tell you.

Libby: But if she's not dead how can she talk to you?

James: I'm dealing with frequencies of energy, sometimes the thoughts are sent very quickly and get mixed up so translations are very difficult.

Libby: Oh, I gotcha. Like a psychic static cling. Believe me, anyone who's ever attended a function with a sock stuck to the back of her dress can identify.

I have to admit I was skeptical but – oh gosh! You know, between you and me and the wall, I always thought I had a bit of a gift too. Wait until I tell you this.

About five years ago I was just about to throw out all my '70's clothes and a very weird, almost spiritual thing came over me. I heard a voice in my head who sounded oddly like Marty Allen and it said "Libby, the minute you throw that stuff out is the minute it will be in fashion again."

Well, I ignored that voice and thousands of dollars later I'm still trying to recreate my old wardrobe!!! Can you believe it? Isn't that spooky? It just shows you! I guess that everyone has the gift inside them, they just need to listen to their inner voice, am I right?

James: Yes, if you buy my book.

Libby: Oh, I just thought that many people might naturally have the gift.

James: No. You need the book.

Libby: Oh, I see. Well thank you James, honestly this has been remarkable. Could you possibly get my grandmother back? Maybe page her? •*HW*•

"I hope the Garden of Paradise still looks nice after she gets her paws on the pruning shears..."

Aging Supermodels: *Their tragic stories in their own words.*

By Sharon Grehan

Linda Seron

I've had one of the longest cover modelling careers in history. I started at 11 and I was gracing top magazine covers all over the world right up until last year when I got a laugh line.

I've heard that most senior models can move on to runway modelling but it's an area that has never interested me. I don't really like airports.

I've always been the 'girl next-door' type so it was in keeping with my image that I would opt for a more traditional (some may say boring!) role.

I married an aging rock star and settled in Mustique with my husband and my two little girls; Messiah and Pebla.

Margo Cartwright

One minute you're hot, the next minute you're not.

Immediately after my career ended, I started my own line of designer clothing. I figured there was a market for women like me so I designed a wonderful line for the six foot, ninety pound woman.

It was so weird, I only sold six outfits! I think I put the chicken before the horse though, so I have a new project coming up that I know is a sure-fire winner. I've been asked to pen "The Ultimate Supermodel Cookbook." Writing is so easy! I just talk and this guy puts it in a book. I wish I'd known that before I wasted all that time in kindergarten.

Clarize

It was hard to think that all my best years were behind me. It took me a couple of months to realize that I just wasn't beautiful anymore, then I went to a Wal-Mart and realized if people can walk around looking like that, then I don't have any thing to be ashamed of.

In a way, I was quite relieved when it was over, there was so much to experience outside of the modelling world. Dance parties, sleep-overs, pillow fights—of course I had experienced all these before, but it is so much more fun to do it with people under 50.

It was also great to go to a BBQ and not slip through the cracks in the deck.

Cheri Simons

I got into the field very early, my hospital baby photo made the cover of *People* and it took off from there.

An unfortunate and tragic genetic accident ended my career early. One minute I'm on top of the world and the next I'm buying stocks in Accutane and Olestra.

It was so very difficult. It is a known fact that beautiful people are very, very nice because people are very, very nice to them. Average people—well average people are dealt with averagely and homely...well you just don't know how rough the world can be until you've crossed the border that leads to the road ugly.

When I hit puberty it was like I exploded. My waistline, my face, my dreams.

My new way of life has been very difficult for me. Where once all I had to say was "Could I have an Evian?" and I would have three people rushing to help me, I now get responses like "who died and made you God?" or "are both your legs broken?" It's been very tough but I know the only way I'll get through it is with courage and surgery. •*HW*•

HW DISPATCH: News for Happy Women

Instant Messaging Causes Cancer

The Centers for Disease Control report that instant messaging has been linked to cancer in laboratory mice. "It wasn't the cancer finding that surprised us so much as how well the mice could type," said Dr. Ferdinand Ellard. "Once introduced to the AOL Instant Messenger, the mice quickly set up buddy lists to exchange tips with their friends in other laboratories throughout the U.S. and Canada." Of the 53 mice involved in the experiment, three developed cancer, a dozen suffered from eyestrain, and about 50 developed a deep-seated hatred of America Online. AOL quickly released a statement claiming that their own studies showed that instant messaging is loaded with antioxidants and contributes to a healthy diet. They also offered the disgruntled mice a CD containing 960 hours of free Internet access with no credit card required. —*E. Hanes*

Seniors Sick Of "Lame-Ass" Entertainment Vow Not To Clap.

Rosedale seniors shocked fans of the Amazing Deluxe All Star Cow Bell Band by refusing to cheer, clap or even nod during their musical performance at the retirement home on Tuesday.

A spokesperson said. "We've sat through 1500 preschool talent shows, 534 recitations, and 62 performances of Patty and her Perky Pekinese. You have to draw the line. We're old, but we're not in hell yet."

Organizers of the event refused to comment on the record about the incident, but one source said, "The next thing they'll want is cable and solid food. Ridiculous."—*S. Grehan*

The Rules of Family: Advice from Donna Corleone

By Pamela Monk

DEAR MADRONE,

I have a busy life, getting my kids everywhere to this and that lesson and practice, you know how it goes, and with everything that goes on, sometimes I get a little behind schedule. Well, I pay good money to this *gavone* of a violin teacher who made a face at me the other day when I brought my Rosemary to group practice a little bit late, so what if they'd started? How can I make him pay?

Disrespected, Bayonne.

Dear Disrespected,

The next time the *palooka* gives you attitude, grab his violin and threaten to smash it unless he gets on his knees and thanks you for your patronage. Then smash it anyway. This will only work if he believes you are going to do worse should he rat you out.

God bless, Donna.

Chapter Seven – July

Herstory: "I Finally Said No"

By Meredith Litt

One woman's courageous journey to self-aggrandizement and unadulterated self-love.

I WAS TWENTY-EIGHT years old when "it" happened. I'd tell you what "it" was, but if I don't save it for the anti-climactic end of my article, I'll have to eliminate about a thousand words of my masterfully written text.

I was married to the love of my life and had just landed a job as the head of the marketing department for a new laxative containing ephedrine (to promote fast, all-natural weight loss). My job was everything to me; I lived, breathed, and slept EpheLax. It was so fulfilling for me to be a wife and a career woman at such a young age; it's an accomplishment that few women have achieved, and I felt like a true heroine for females everywhere. In fact, I knew I was.

The problem was that John, my husband, disagreed wholeheartedly. As I pounded out marketing proposals on my laptop until the early morning hours, he took on a selfishness that made him almost unrecognizable to me. He began to ask questions like: "Honey, when are you going to get off the computer so that we can spend some time together?" and "I miss you. Please take some time off of work for our one-year anniversary." To be frank, I knew then that our marriage was doomed to fail. How could I stay married to a man who didn't respect my career and, moreover, my irreplaceable contribution to womankind?

One day, as I arrived home from a twelve-hour day in meetings for a new ad campaign, John looked at me with sad eyes and offered one final plea: "It's been months since you've so much as kissed me. Please, take the weekend off so that I can show you how much I love you."

I was furious. How could he be so selfish? I was about to launch a campaign for EpheLax that would innovate laxative advertisement as the world knew it and make it possible for overweight women everywhere to lose weight and stay regular simultaneously. My efforts were not to be undermined by ridiculous declarations of love and insensitive requests for time off. Looking at him as tears filled his eyes, I wondered how I could have married a man so fixated on himself.

> *"...I felt like a true heroine for females everywhere. In fact, I knew I was."*

It was that day that I finally did it. That word, which had been simmering within my psyche for years, finally effervesced to the surface. That day, I told John, "No." I felt empowered as I continued with a request for a divorce, having finally realized that he could never fulfill my needs.

Ladies, I know that you all suffer from moments of weakness. Your love for your partners may inspire temporary lapses in logic, causing you to prioritize your spouse first and yourself last. Never fall into this trap like I did. Empower yourself. Take the first step, and never look back. It's not about who gets hurt along the way, but, ultimately, about satisfying your own needs. If I can do it, anyone can. •*HW*•

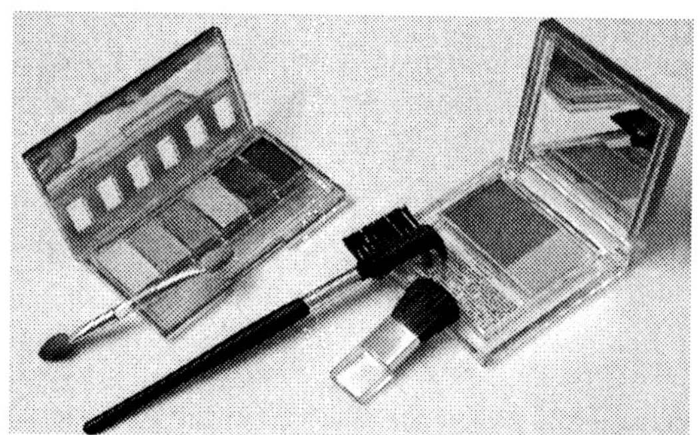

Summer Cosmetic Must-Haves!

By Elizabeth Hanes

Don't brand yourself hopelessly unhip by leaving the house without these essential new cosmetics.

1. *Navel foundation.* Even if your navel is naturally beautiful, you can improve its appearance simply by applying a little navel foundation with a triangular sponge. We like Bobbi Brown's "Naturally Navel" and Cover Girl's "Beautiful Belly Button."

2. *Shoulderblade shadow.* If your idea of weightlifting is carrying your lunch to work, chances are you could use some toning up – or better yet the illusion of it! Use a large makeup brush to apply shoulderblade shadow below and between your shoulderblades to create contours that give the illusion of muscle tone. You'll look sex-sational at the beach! We like Max Factor's "Bold Blade" and Maybelline's "ShadowSexy for Shoulderblades."

3. *Flavoured ankle rouge.* Drive your man wild by accentuating that sexy dimple on the inside of your ankle. Next time you wear sandals, just blend on a dab of flavoured ankle rouge and watch his mouth water in sensual anticipation! The taste adds a whole new dimension to toe-sucking. We like Lancome's "Ankle Sensuelle" (available in green apple and bubblegum flavours) and Estee Lauder's "Foot Licks" (cherry, watermelon, and orange.)

4. *Knee concealer.* Let's face it: for most of us, our knees are not our most

attractive feature. Knee concealer solves that problem! Apply generously, and the concealer gives your knees a sleek, plastic look - like a Barbie doll! Best of all, the new polymer-based formulations won't crack when you bend, like the old types did. We like Clinique's "Patella Plastique" and Avon's "Naturally Plastic for Knees."

5. *Bikini area mascara.* If you accidentally overdid your home bikini wax, don't fret. Just apply several coats of specially-formulated bikini area mascara to the remaining hair to create fuller, thicker pubes. Best of all, most formulas are waterproof - no embarrassing running after a nice swim! For a walk on the wild side, try mascara in purple, blue, and green shades! We like Revlon's "Bikini-scara Extraordinaire" and Guerlain's "Great Pubes Mascara." •*HW*•

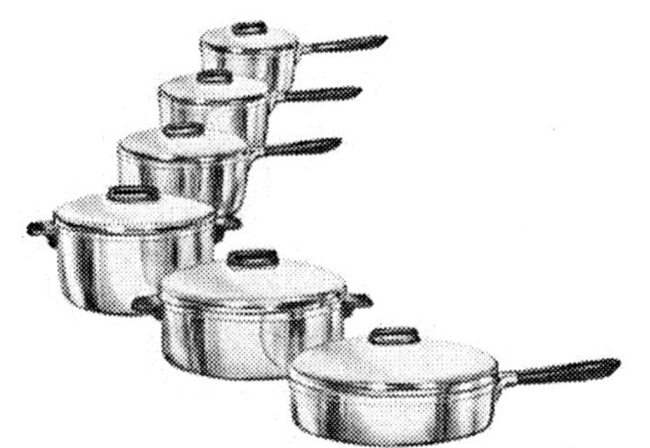

Calphalon, My Lovely

By Elaine Langlois

YOU FINALLY HAVE that perfect six-figure kitchen. So the next question becomes, what is the *right* sort of cookware for you to use? Is there any other choice? The cookware of the millennium, ladies, is Calphalon.

Why Calphalon? Well, first off, Calphalon is *expensive.* We take pride in saying that a starter set almost certainly costs more than the pots and pans of all your friends put together. It is also clearly recognizable from a distance as Calphalon, so it will be clear to them that you can afford the best.

Calphalon has a number of features that set it apart from other fine cookware. For instance, it is as heavy as cast iron, the cookware of choice of our ancestors. So you can see that it takes a special kind of woman to *handle* Calphalon. In an emergency, Calphalon can be used for self-defense. We know personally of a case of robbery foiled by a woman armed only with our Omelette Pan.

Another distinctive feature of Calphalon is that non-stick cooking sprays are best not used with it. These sprays can cause a gummy residue to build up on the surface of your pan. In cookware, as in life, *surface* is what really matters. Foods will not stick to your Calphalon if you follow these simple steps:

1. Allow foods to warm slightly (this is best accomplished by *taking them out of the*

refrigerator).

2. Preheat your pan over medium heat. Test it by tapping it with your fingers. If it raises blisters, your pan is ready. Alternatively, use a stick of butter to coat the inside of the pan *(take the wrapper off first*). If the butter immediately turns brown and sets off the smoke detector, the pan is *too hot*. Your next step should be to *turn the heat down*.

3. Keep your cookware scrupulously clean (more on this below). For assistance, we suggest our online tutorial, "How Can I Tell if My Calphalon Is Clean?"

You will need to add a tablespoon of oil or butter when cooking with most Calphalon. We are sure from what we know of you that you will not feel threatened by this. Nutritionists are the first to admit that we need some fat in our lives. An extra mile on the treadmill should cover it.

At a suggested retail price of $100 for the Everyday Pan, your Calphalon is an investment. Treat it so. We ask that you not stack Calphalon on Calphalon, nor let it associate too closely with other types of pots and pans.

Calphalon is tough, yet tender. *Do not put it through the dishwasher*. This will void your Lifetime Warranty and cause us intense personal pain. To clean non-stick Calphalon, gently massage it with Q-Tips and baby oil. For Calphalon with hard-anodized aluminum or stainless steel surfaces, scrub vigorously with #3 steel wool and a paste composed of ordinary household soap and feldspar *(wear leather gloves*). This is a good opportunity to catch up on your books on tape and develop those upper-arm muscles. Disparaging remarks, such as "How long is it going to take to get this wretched pot clean?" certainly will not help. For stubborn stains, hooking the pan onto the back of your SUV and driving through a carwash should yield good results.

So, when you're ready for cookware that makes a statement about your material success, choose Calphalon. We've heard our competitors running down the features of each other's cookware. We don't engage in that kind of negative advertising. In fact, it strikes us as (dare we say it?) the pot calling the kettle black. Ho! Don't say we don't have a sense of humour here at Calphalon. •*HW*•

Herstory: Confessions of a Trophy Wife
By Maria Dolan as told to Sharon Grehan

I met Brad 20 years ago when I was 19. I was working as an aerobics instructor at Club Inferno and he was a type A trying to get into shape.

It went the way most love stories do: he loved the way I looked in Lycra and I loved the way he looked in his Jag.

It was a long time before we were able to be married because he had some loose ends to tie up, like his wife and three kids, but finally I was wed to the man of my dreams.

We were married for eighteen years when I started to sense something was wrong.

Brad worked very hard. He had to work every night and was forced to go on business trips every weekend so I didn't think that he would have time for an affair, but there were tiny tell-tale signs that things were going on.

Tiny things like tampons in his glovebox and a brassiere stuffed behind the backseat, lipstick on his underpants.

I didn't want to doubt Brad but I had to confront him when I caught him naked in bed with his ex-wife's babysitter Diane.

Two hours after he got back from driving her home, I told him of my suspicions.

He told me that Diane was interested in purchasing a Sealy Posturepedic and that she'd never slept naked on cotton sheets before. The tampons were for his ears, the lipstick was for luck and the brassiere was there for me in case of emergency.

I felt terrible for doubting him and tried to make it up to him by making up funny limericks and making my birthmark smile. But I became suspicious again after he came in one night and said "I don't love you anymore. I'm moving in with Diane."

When Brad moved out the next day I had a hunch that all was not right in my personal paradise. I didn't hear from Brad for a week and his dinners were getting really cold.

I found Diane's number and got up the nerve to call him. He said that he couldn't talk because he had lost his voice but I was not to be denied I had to say what was on my mind.

I told him that I was nothing without him and he agreed but he still was not coming home.

I was shattered. I spent endless days just wandering around the house in my bathrobe weeping and letting my roots show until one day I caught sight of myself in the mirror. Everything became clear.

I had let myself get old.

I'd always exercised because Brad hated any percentage of body fat and I went to the

"I called his ex-wife to tell her what he had done to me..."

hairdresser every day with a frosting once a week. I had weekly facials and monthly peels but still I had failed.

I took a long hard look in the mirror. I saw the crow's feet around my eyes and the pouch under my chin. My body was slender but the flesh was not as tight and wrinkles had appeared.

Confronted with this grotesque apparition I was energized and very fortunate to have a plastic surgeon who could handle emergencies

While recovering, I memorized jokes and caught up on my soaps—all the things I didn't have time for when I was with Brad because I was busy shopping.

At the end of six weeks I looked as I did 20 years before only a little more surprised.

Brad started to call me once he got his voice back because he wanted some of his things back, like some personal papers, his clothes and the house, but I ignored his calls and his lawyer's calls until I was ready for the unveiling.

Once the bruises healed I invited Brad over. I ordered in a sumptuous feast and dreamed of our romantic reunion, but Brad asked if he could get it to take-out as Diane was waiting out front in the car.

I fumed as I stuffed the food in plastic containers. *Enough,* I swore to myself. *Enough.*

I did nothing to deserve this. I was well groomed every day of my life. I watched the staff keep the house clean and made witty comments at cocktail parties. What more could a man want?

Brad wanted someone younger.

I called his ex-wife to tell her what he had done to me but instead of commiserating she just laughed hysterically. (I don't understand why women won't help each other. She was an old skank anyway but she didn't have to be so cold.)

I was desperate and alone. I needed some time for quiet contemplation so I went for a bikini wax. While she ripped the hair out, I looked deep within.

All this time I thought looking beautiful and being able to wear just about anything was enough—it wasn't. I probed further and realized that I had devoted so much time to Brad and my personal appearance that I had left no time for improving my inner self. I was...empty.

Oh, well I didn't want to dwell on what I couldn't change so I paid the aesthetician and bought some gum.

I sued Brad for everything I could but I ended up with a piddly allowance that wouldn't even keep me in facial peels.

I knew that I would have to find a way to survive, so I cruised the nightspots but the crowds were so young that I felt completely out of place.

I started going to lounge bars out by the airport but still love and security eluded me. The men arriving at the airport were all married, which wasn't a problem, the problem was they were looking for someone even younger than me. Out of desperation I finally ended up attending lawn bowling tournaments.

That was the smartest thing I ever did.

I met an adorable man named Edward and we were married three weeks after we met. It was a lovely service. Edward looked so handsome as they wheeled him down the aisle and I looked a thousand times better than his great-granddaughter who was my bridesmaid.

Edward and I are blissfully happy. I visit him every other week in the home and let him feel my new breasts.

As I write this, I am watching the sunset from the deck of my beach house. I sometimes look back on my journey, the twelve weeks of suffering and misery, and I realize how much I've grown. I watch the news and when I see wars in foreign countries and famine. I feel empathy and depending on whether or not I'm wearing mascara I sometimes share a tear for my brothers and sisters.

I wouldn't wish those weeks of misery on anybody except Brad, Diane and his ex-wife.

I have triumphed. •*HW*•

QUIZ: Are You in Labour?

by Elizabeth Hanes

You've suffered through nine months of vomiting, binge eating and crying jags. Now, with your belly as big as a barn, you just want to get this pregnancy over with. At last, you feel a cramp and rush to the hospital only to find out you've been fooled by "false labour." So how can you tell when those abdominal pains are the real deal?

First, disregard all that scientific mumbo-jumbo about "dilation" and "mucous quality." That hocus-pocus is a source of much misinformation in the world of feminine medical care. The fact is, certain events can accurately predict the onset of true labour. Take our quiz and tally your score to see how close you are to making that "special delivery." •*HW*•

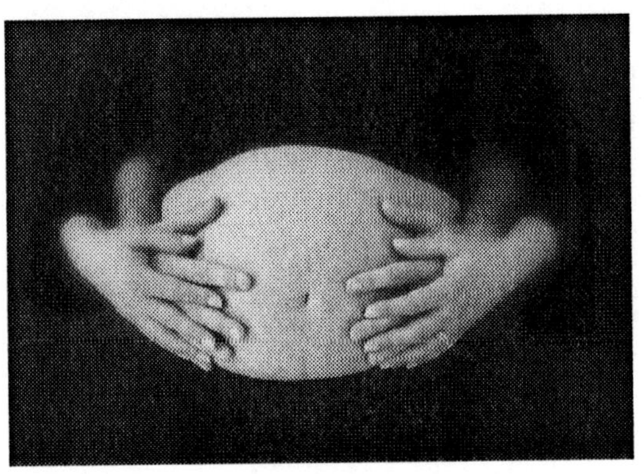

QUIZ

1. Is your husband away on a "quick" business trip?

___ Yes (8 points)

___ No (-1 point)

2. Did you decide to take a relaxing drive in the country and now find yourself stranded on the side of the road with a flat tire?

___ Yes (9 points. Add 1 point if your cell phone battery is dead.)

___ No (-6 points)

3. Did you just buy $400 worth of new maternity clothes because the doctor assured you on your last visit that your labour was still "quite a ways off"?

___ Yes (12 points)

___ No (-16 and add 7 points)

4. Is your house full of 20 rambunctious Girl Scouts because it's your day to host the troop?

___ Yes (3 Add 1 point for each parent you're unable to reach by telephone.)

___ No (-6 points)

5. Are you camping at a remote site, outside your cell phone calling area?

___ Yes (2 points)

___ No (-1 point)

6. Did your toddler accidentally fall and knock her tooth out just as your young son walked through the door announcing he thinks his arm is broken?

___ Yes (11 points)

___ No (-5 points)

7. Is there a thunderstorm raging?

___ Yes (13 points. Add 1 point if you're also under a Tornado Watch. Add 3 points if a tornado has just touched down on the edge of town or near the hospital.)

___ No (-1 point)

8. Are you in a Boeing 747, cruising at 30,000 feet?

___ Yes (7 points)

___ No (-23 points)

9. Did you rent a $3,000 designer gown to wear to an awards ceremony because your water has "never broken on its own before"?

___ Yes (2 points)

___ No (-9 points)

10. Are you on holiday, in a foreign country, at a large amusement park, relying on a phrasebook because you don't exactly speak the language?

___ Yes (19 points. Add 3 points if you've just boarded "the world's longest rollercoaster.")

___ No (-17 points)

SCORING:

8-15+ - You're so in labour you should form a union.

4-7 - You're probably in labour and also have a past history of delivering a child in the back seat of a taxi.

1-3 - If you take the quiz again in 2 hours and your score improves, start boiling water and tearing sheets into strips.

Miracle Drugs and Diets

By Sharon Grehan

WE HEAR IT ALL the time, medical professionals pooh-poohing new diets and pills, telling us the only way to lose weight is to eat less and exercise blah, blah, blah. But we discovered we have something that the medical community doesn't have—desperate hope!

We asked our readers to give us their success stories; maybe you will find the right miracle cure for you!

Drugs:

Redux

I had to gain 20 pounds to be a candidate for the drug but it was worth it!! The dry mouth was gone in only 6 weeks and I was able to talk and answer the phone and everything. I'm drowsy a lot of the time at work but I put a cushion in front of my keyboard to keep from bruising. I have shortness of breath, chest pain, fainting, swelling of the legs, ankles, and feet but I feel great!!!

I've lost ten pounds so far!

Julie Senton

Xenical

Xenical blocks one third of the fat I eat. I can still indulge in ice-cream sundaes and potato chips with absolutely no guilt!!!

The oily discharge is off-putting at first and the inability to control bowel movements has caused much hilarity in our house. But what do a few extra loads of laundry and being housebound compare to melting off the pounds!

I am so looking forward to the day I've lost all the weight and I can leave the house to go clothes shopping!

Maggie Cooper

Phenylpropanolamine

I had a little bit of bleeding into the brain but I lost a ton of weight in the hospital. Once I regain the use of my right arm I'm going to pursue my dream of acting—something I couldn't even think about when I was fat! Whooo hoooo!

Vanessa Hill

Herbal Remedies:

Cellasene

I just wanted to get rid of my cream cheese thighs so Cellasene is an answer to my prayer! It's supposed to increase blood circulation, reduce fluid build-up, stimulate metabolism and reduce localized fats.

It's a win/win situation to me because if it doesn't work I can join the class action lawsuit!

Annette Gaudet

Metabolife

This is a miracle drug. I've lost 12 pounds in three weeks. I've had a few minor side effects like stomach cramping, panic attacks, nervous shakes, hallucinations, two seizures and I may not be able to drive anymore, but by the summer I will finally be able to wear a bathing suit again!

Megan Anderson

Ephedra
Editor's Note:
Suze Longsford was supposed to tell us about her experience with Ephedra but she is still in intensive care. Get Well Soon Suze! Kisses!

Diets:

Atkins' Diet Low Carb
I've been on this diet for 9 months. People look at me in awe when I order steak and eggs for breakfast and no one can believe that I have lost so much weight eating prime rib for lunch!
I'm still a little constipated, nauseated, weak, dehydrated, and my kidneys are failing but I repeat: I can have steak for breakfast!
Annie Conner

Weight Watchers
I have successfully lost all my excess weight and kept it off for good - twelve times!!! The people are nice and the 1-2-3 program takes away the thinking. I've met many friends over the twenty years I've been going. Whenever I go back it's just like old-home week. This program really works every single time.
Cindy Patterson
•*HW*•

Let Your Apron be Your Smile
By Sarah W. Szucs

NO MATTER WHAT they're saying on talk radio there is one thing that cannot be denied—women love aprons. A woman standing at attention by her hearth in a cleanly pressed apron says, "I am ready to work." It also says, "I will not allow my outfit to be soiled by dust nor dough."

A woman's apron can express a dozen moods. It can be her smile, or it can be her wrath. But most often it is her smile. In grandma's day aprons were hard to come by, and what cloth coverings could be found were unbelievably boring. Thank goodness that in this progressive age, there is an apron for each stop on every woman's hectic schedule.

Starting your day with a bright new apron is as natural as a fresh brewed pot of coffee. It lets your family and neighbours know that the sunrise shift has begun! Good suggestions for your morning apron include bright, cheerful colours and happy patterns. Perhaps polka dots in fun, contrasting colours are your style. Light-hearted images of cockadoodling roosters or animated breakfast foods are always favorites.

The lunch apron is a quieter, less playful apron. It says, "I'm ready for a nap." Small prints are fine, but be sure to choose eye-soothing colours such as pale blue or dark green. If your midday apron should have animated lunch foods be sure their eyes are half-closed. They might also be propped against a large sleepy-faced clock to further emphasize the point of impending nap time.

The dinner apron says, "I am rested and ready to play." However, this apron is not only functional but also dressy and alluring. Good colour choices for this garment include rich red, elegant white or sophisticated black. Fabrics should be luxurious. See-through organza, glamorous lamé and fancy lace are all excellent foundations for the breathtaking apron every woman wants to wear. The shape of this apron is quite form fitting at the bodice and starched breast darts are a must. The skirt of this apron is gathered at the waist with a large satin bow and opening to a heavily ruffled skirt. Using a petticoat or peplum underneath is strongly suggested to enhance this formal look. And it goes without saying that wearing a corset is common sense.

You may ask, "As this dinner apron is very much like a negligee could it is also be suitable for the boudoir?" In a word, yes! An apron is always welcome behind the closed doors of the bedroom. It is suggested that the bedroom apron is most efficient if paired with an appropriate floor length robe and turban.

And there you have it - 24 hours worth of letting your apron be your smile. And remember, when your apron does the smiling it's one less chore on your "to do" list. •*HW*•

Choice: Is it Killing us? A HW Special Report

By Sharon Grehan

NORTH AMERICANS ARE becoming fatter, lazier, and dumber according to a study released today by the National Organization for Sensible Youth (NOSY). The study reveals that freedom of choice is killing us. Not only is there an obesity epidemic but the report finds that our minds are turning to jelly as the result of TV.

The study also found that the average North American consumes over 245 gallons of soda per year, 615 burgers and 417 orders of fries. As well, North Americans average over 10½ hours of television watching per day and when quizzed, only 3% knew where the sun was.

The report claims the resulting health care and supplemental educational costs are in the "bajillions" of dollars.

The conclusion? There is a definite correlation between choice and death. Left to their own devices, North Americans will invariably make harmful or as the study states "wrong" choices. Based on these results, NOSY will lobby congress to pass a bill that will initially restrict and ultimately prohibit choice.

Lauren Quimby, centre spokesperson and founder said "We must eliminate choice. It is the only way to protect our youth. Children are our future. It's too late to save the adults but it is our duty to protect the young."

Quimby, a former hand model, launched NOSY in the fall of 2000 after noticing very few people thought as she did. Quimby, well known in her community for getting a ban on skateboards and funny T-shirts, was encouraged by her curling club to take her organizational talents one step further. She was inspired by the efforts of The Center for Science in the Public Interest which has been pushing for a fat tax (also known as the "Twinkie Tax"), a ban on soda pop, and perfume as well as a "No See TV" week.

"We have a three-stage plan. Once we build awareness and garner public support there will be no stopping us. Our first phase calls for a ban on high-heel shoes, sitcoms, violence in dreams, and yellow, then we'll move on to phase two where the targets will be cell phones, power lines, microwaves, electric blankets, and canned food."

Socio-cultural anthropologist Myra Boyle Watson, a general complainer and wrecker of good times pooh-poohed the study. "This is garbage. There are so many holes in this I don't know where to begin. What qualifications does Ms. Quimby have?"

Quimby said in response, "I don't think you need to hold a degree in order to be right. If Myra Boyle Watson doesn't care about the children, we do. Besides, the CSPI has a ton of people who are doctors and stuff and they're saying basically the same thing I am, but with more words."

While Quimby is behind the CSPI and other organizations, she feels that they are a trifle soft. Instead of imposing a fat tax, Quimby suggests going one step further and making fast food illegal. "That's in our third phase. The 'If you can't have it you won't be tempted' phase.

"Look at it this way, you can't walk into a drug store and say 'Gee, what would make me feel better, an aspirin or some heroin?' You don't do that because heroin isn't available in the drugstore. If it were, then (although we haven't actually done a study) 97% of people would choose heroin. I think the figures speak for themselves."

At a television press conference, Quimby stated that a complete TV ban should be part of the third phase of NOSY's plan.

"Dr. Nestle and Dr. Jacobson, who are my personal heroes next to Mother Teresa and John Stossel, stated in the Public Health Reports: 'Television is an increasingly well-established risk factor for obesity and its health consequences... The Surgeon General could announce a campaign to reduce television watching.'

"That's an example of good, or *right* thinking," says Quimby "but once again it's rather soft. Reducing TV time won't do anything, but *banning* TV will. We'd also like to crack down on the Internet. I don't have a computer myself but I know for a fact that the Internet is nothing but a haven for pornographers.

"The CPSI is doing great things but I firmly believe NOSY can do better."

Watson said, "Sorry, I can't answer any more questions. I have an image of kids buying black market Happy Meals."•*HW*•

HW DISPATCH: News for Happy Women

Montana Woman Concedes Defeat
Single mother Carolyn Fishburn of Anaconda, Montana, held a news conference Tuesday night to concede defeat in her bid to take control of her household. "I ran a good campaign," Fishburn read from a prepared statement, "but, ultimately, I could not muster enough votes to maintain my seat as home governor." Fishburn went on to blame Nintendo and Fox television, specifically *The Simpsons* program, for her defeat. "My platform of sit-down family dinners, wholesome values, and participation in extracurricular activities fell flat with my children," she admitted. The five Fishburn children echoed their mother's sentiments. "We really only want to eat cookies and play video games," said 14-year-old Johnny, the eldest, acting as spokesman for the family. "When we went to the polls, we seized our opportunity to oust the incumbent and install new leadership." Carolyn Fishburn, who was running unopposed, also blamed her 8-year-old daughter for the election-day loss. "Julie represented the swing vote, and I thought I had her support sewn up when I agreed to let her wear a princess costume for Halloween. Obviously, she betrayed me, and I won't soon forget it." It's unclear who will now lead the Fishburn family. Political pundits have named Homer Simpson and Crash Bandicoot as the frontrunners. —*E. Hane*

The Rules of Family: Advice from Donna Corleone
By Pamela Monk

DEAR MADRONE,
My next door neighbor is always bragging about her recipe for peach cobbler. Which I can swear to you tastes like cardboard slathered with cheap jelly. So the other day, I was finally sick and tired of pretending she was Betty frigging Crocker , so I took a piece and left it on the ground for the dog, who wouldn't touch it. So now she won't speak to me. What do I do? Can I help it if the dog speaks truth? *Too honest in LaVinia*

Dear Honest
Count yourself lucky. A true friend understands true friends. If she can't take this little helpful criticism how will she handle it when things go south? Like when she takes said pie to the pot luck and she has to take the pie back with just a slice or two gone, or worse people take it but leave it on their plates after one bite only. You should try this with all of your friends, and see which remain in your camp. That will tell you something, you need to know who is stand up and who isn't going to have your back at the bake sale.
God bless, Donna

Chapter Eight – August

What To Do With All Those "Friends" Once You've Caught A Man

By Sarah W. Szucs

THEY CALL YOU IN the middle of the night. They look at you with hungry eyes and slumping posture. They are pathetic. They are your friends. You, however, have been kissed by the arrow of Cupid - and walk hand in hand with the handsomely strong man whom you love. Can't your friends be friends enough to see that you are too much in love to be bothered with their pettiness? What in this great green earth could be the motivation for these hangers on? A true friend would not keep interrupting your romantic bliss to remind you of the horrors of being single with phone calls to go places and do things. What for? You aren't shopping anymore.

After a while it becomes obvious—they are after your man. You think perhaps you should throw them a bone and fix them up with one of your man's friends. But what if that romantic relationship soured? Then they would only blame you and it could put an awkward strain on your friendship. Worse yet, what if their relationship lasted longer than your present one? Then you'd be the dreary old maid haunting them all the time! Better put that idea to rest, now.

Sadly, friendship is work. And it is your unfortunate duty to have to socialize with your friends on occasion. But keep these singletons at arms length (see previous discussion "…it becomes obvious—they are after your man"). And, heaven forbid, should you ever be single again you will need comfortable shoulders to fall back on! Invest your time with them prudently—perhaps the time that your sweetheart has to work late or cannot canoodle with you for whatever reason.

Consider this precious time of yours as more "charity work" than social outing. Pretend that you are being called by a higher power to bestow the very strength and wisdom that helped you hog-tie Cupid onto these waif-ish castoffs. Nod knowingly, and appropriately, as they tearfully confess another romantic failure to you. You are their pillar of strength and their beacon of hope. Holding you in such high regard, you can do no wrong in their eyes. Be blunt, and critical, as needed. That's what friends do.

And they certainly won't mind if throughout the evening you check in with your love of a lifetime with intimate cell phone calls and cutesy text messages. The poor single dear may need this time to dab those tears that have been clinging to her eyelashes for the previous forty minutes and perhaps even re-read an old tattered love note. While you're on the phone make sure you keep your own love life sizzling by speaking in baby talk and using affectionate pet names. Be sure to finish every conversation with something along the lines of how lucky you are to have found your soul mate because if you had to be single in today's market you'd want to kill yourself.

After a few hours of this hand holding you are free to flee back to your mate. Run like the wind before she finds more tissue. Once you are back in the arms of your man-passion, you feel in his trembling grip he has also visited the ghost of single-hood past. Somehow this horror has rekindled your love with a determination to make this relationship work, no matter what. And best of all, you feel good that you have paid your "friendship dues" and won't need to see those single souls again for at least a few weeks. You'll see them much sooner, of course, if your relationship with "Mr. Poohbear" sours. •*HW*•

"If you must *walk you should draw attention away from the no-no nethers."*

Swimsuit Season!

By Sharon Grehan

How to minimize the flab and maximize the Fab!

If the thought of putting on a swimsuit has caused you hand-wringing, night-sweats and irrational behaviour, then despair no more! Our sassy, savvy swimsuit stylists have taken the most common figure flaws and devised ways for even the most bovine bather to take advantage of Mother Nature's bathtub!!!

Problem Area: Butt
Solution: Sitting is recommended. Lots and lots of sitting. Arrange beach props around you. Umbrellas, coolers, sleeping infants all make wonderful tools for camouflage. If you *must* walk you should draw attention away from the no-no nethers. A large tattoo of a dragon on your shoulderblades, a bowl of fruit on your head, a parrot on your shoulder—any one of these will draw the eyeball up, up and away!
Tip: Ripe fruit is not recommended and the parrot should be tame.

Problem Area: Thighs
Solution: Set your alarm for 5:30. Artfully arrange a towel or, depending on the size of the problem area, a king sized bed sheet around the offending region. That will get you from the car to the sand.

Once there, dig a trench approx. five inches or twenty-five centimetres deep (try not to dig deeper than that as you might require a building permit.) Lie down and once your thighs have completely spread out (this could take a few minutes) have your friends cover the excess you with a layer of sand. With a little work you can literally get the sculpted curves you've always dreamed off!

Tip: Best to have loads of sunscreen on hand and avoid liquids unless the trench is over five inches deep.

Problem Area: Upper Arm Sag

Solution: Water wings would provide the most noticeable results as would a cardigan but the most practical solution is two-sided carpet tape applied to the side of your bathing suit. Once in place hold arms at your side until arms have bonded to the suit.

Tip: Avoid pointing, invest in a long straw and you might want to remove tape before swimming.

Problem Area: Bulging Tummy

Solution: The manufacturers for years dealt with this problem by making cunning little ruffle-skirted numbers. Now however, the jig is up! The public has now caught on to the fact that a skirt on your bathing suit means you've never met a Krispy Kreme you didn't like.

The miracle cure? A humble beach ball! Yes this much maligned pleasure tool can easily hide last winter's Ben & Jerry deposits. Take a 17" diameter or 36" (again depending on the expanse) beach ball. With both hands bring the ball up in front of you 3 inches below the breastbone and hold it out ¼ inch away from your chest. It is very important that the measurements be exact. Keep it there until you go home.

If you have limited upper arm strength you might want to try the pregnancy ploy. Purchase a T-shirt that announces your condition like the hilarious classic T "baby on board" and watch as the glances from strangers turn from disdain to delight.

Tip: If you go for the beach ball option you might want to purchase a high-power water pistol to discourage enthusiastic toddlers and if you decide the pregnancy option is best for you avoid smoking and drinking alcoholic beverages in front of the other beach patrons. •*HW*•

Raising Your Ungifted Child

By Elizabeth Hanes

THE WORLD ABOUNDS with resources for nurturing the overbearing talents of the gifted child or, conversely, the "slow" child. If you had the good fortune to spawn a prodigy, endless learning centres and mentors spring from nowhere to exploit your child's talent while bringing it to fruition, doubtlessly garnering themselves and you a mountain of lucre in the process. If, on the other hand, your child is seriously learning-disabled (as we politely call it these days), dozens of do-gooders will be more than happy to devote their boundless time and energy into molding your child into a productive member of society.

But what if you're not so lucky? What if your child falls in that daunting range of IQ between "dullard" and "average"? Not so stupid as to be learning-disabled, but certainly well below average, and nowhere within spitting distance of genius? Take heart; all is not lost. With a few well-thought-out strategies, you can transform your child's prospects from "Do you want fries with that?" to "Can I count on your support to make this season's charity ball a success?"

Dealing with a vacuous girl is much more challenging than rearing a dull-witted boy. It's not that fewer boys are dullards, it's just that this problem was conquered long ago through the "Old Boys' Network." All one must do for the simple-minded boy is ensure that rich Uncle Ralph or dear friend of the family Austin reserves a place at the executive level of the family business, where the young man can reap a six-figure salary while doing fairly little damage to the company's interests. Heavens, a dull-witted boy might even grow up to be President! Girls, on the other hand, require a bit more finessing.

Trophy wifedom obviously should be the goal. You must begin cultivating superficiality in your daughter from an early age. Forget about formal education. You can teach her to read and write at home, and if she marries as well as expected, she'll have no use for arithmetic. Besides, stimulating her intellect would be stressful, and worry lines can begin appearing as early as age five. She'll never land a man that way! Instead, teach her the practical skills she'll need to succeed in life. Show her how to apply makeup at age three, when her motor skills have sufficiently developed. By age five, she must be adept at walking in 4" heels. Beauty pageants, of course, are absolutely necessary to her training. Lightening her hair, plucking her eyebrows, waxing her legs: all of this should be *de rigeuer* before she's nine.

Age twelve is not too early to begin shopping her around for a prospective mate. We're not suggesting she actually marry that young, but long betrothals provide an opportunity for priming the money siphon and tucking away currency in off-shore bank accounts. Another advantage to the long engagement is

> *"Age twelve is not too early to begin shopping her around for a prospective mate."*

that should the elderly gentleman (i.e.: fiancé) kick the bucket, your daughter will already have accumulated quite an array of beautiful and expensive baubles, which are hers to keep. A lovely "parting gift," as it were.

Your dim-witted child also must learn how to express herself appropriately. She must always appear cheerful and perky, except during sad movies, operas, and funerals, when she must cry daintily and elegantly. She should be aware of current events and her stand on them. Fortunately, the main current events never change, so she can formulate her opinion at an early age and keep voicing it for the rest of her days. Topics to concentrate on are: homelessness, poverty (especially starving children in third-world countries), and world peace. Memorizing a few choice phrases, such as, "I believe each of us needs to reach out and build a bridge to the homeless and the poverty-stricken in order to bring about world peace," will also serve her nicely during the Miss America pageant. These sorts of statements, delivered in a breathy, high-pitched voice, are sure-fire husband magnets!

Obviously, not all dull-witted girls are going to grow up to be Pamela Anderson. You must accept your child's limitations, after all. However, with a little extra effort from you, perhaps some acting classes and plastic surgery, your ungifted child can, indeed, become a decorative, if not productive, member of society. •*HW*•

The Sheep Shearer's Workout

By Sharon Grehan

This routine is supreme in its simplicity. Follow this workout everyday for the next 21 days and you'll go from yuck to yowie in no time!

What you will need:

- Handpieces, combs and cutters (optional)
- A grinder (optional)
- A catching pen (optional)
- A counting out pen (optional)
- 12 sheep per day. (required)

First Step

Do some simple stretching exercises as a warm-up--Do not skip this step.

Second Step

Round up the sheep in the catching pen. Be very careful not to hurt your back. Grab the sheep and turn its head around until it drops in front of you. Using your arms pull the sheep up.

Third Step

Using the comb and cutter shear the wool in a set pattern. Be very careful not to nick the scrotum of the sheep (if male) or the teats of a ewe (if female). This does not affect the fitness aspect but it can be very icky.

Fourth Step

Repeat previous steps, release the sheep into the counting pen or the street if you live in an apartment, gather the wool, spin the fleece into yarn, and whip up a yummy sweater for yourself!

That's all there is to it!!!

Tips

- If you cannot find sheep, large dogs will do nicely--just don't shear or slaughter them because dogs are cute.
- A bedroom or den doubles nicely as a holding pen if you live in an apartment.
- Have plenty of garbage bags laid out on the floor. Sheep can be very, very nervous.

Repair Your Own Transmission and Make 3½ Dozen Maple Butter Cookies

The Perfect HW Afternoon!

By Sharon Grehan

What you will need:

- Tools, lots of them.
- 1 cup unsalted butter
- Transmission system
- ¼ cup sugar
- Valve body recalibration kit
- 1 tsp. maple extract or flavoring
- Super pump
- ¼ cup brown sugar
- Torque converter
- Pinch of salt
- Thread-locking compounds
- 1 large egg
- Transmission assembly-lube
- 2¼ cups all-purpose flour
- Transmission fluid
- Red and green decorator sugars, frosting or blanched whole almonds

Preheat oven to 175°C (350°F) degrees.

Raise your car—do not attempt to do this yourself cars are very heavy. You will probably need a jack.

Cream butter, sugar, maple extract, brown sugar, salt and egg yolk with electric mixer until smooth.

Clean any yucky stuff off the transmission and then drain the transmission fluid (the car should be turned off and parked.)

Gradually beat in flour.

Remove the transmission (it is the big thing underneath the car.)

Wrap dough in plastic wrap; refrigerate for 1 hour to let flavours blend.

Remove the torque converter and put it upside down on top of a bucket to drain out old transmission fluid (Note: Make sure the bucket is smaller than the torque converter or it will repeatedly fall in.)

Grease a baking sheet or use parchment paper.

Disassemble the transmission, try to remember where everything goes. We find jolly songs like "the hip bone's connected to the knee-bone" are great memory triggers but since a transmission does not have a hip bone you might have to change the lyrics.

Remove all the old gaskets and seals, and throw them in the dishwasher.

Roll out dough on lightly floured surface to 3 mm (1/8 inch) thickness. (You may want to wash your hands)

Replace all of the bushings in the transmission. You will need a special tool but a toothbrush might come in handy. (Be careful to rinse it thoroughly before you use it again!) Reassemble the transmission and lubricate all the new seals. (You will be glad you took the time to write that song!) Use a torque wrench and tighten all hardware to the manufacturers specifications then recalibrate the valve body for the type of application you need. If you don't know what that means go onto the next step.

Install the modified valve body to the transmission.

Cut into desired shapes using holiday cookie cutters.

Find the transmission's input shaft and place the torque converter which has been filled with automatic transmission fluid. There are a few sets of thingamajigs that have to engage so you may find rotating the converter helps.

Place on lightly greased cookie sheets. Sprinkle with decorator sugars, or press almonds into centre of cookies.

Flush-out the transmission oil-cooler lines.

Bake for 12 to 15 minutes.

Install the transmission and add automatic transmission fluid, start the engine and take it for a test drive. Be sure to remove the jack first and take it out of park.

If anything falls out or the car won't go, push it over a cliff or embankment. (Only do this if you are insured).

Take the cookies out of the oven, allow them to cool and voila!!!! That's all there is to it! •*HW*•

Must Reads For Fall

By Elaine Langlois

THE SUMMER MOVIE blockbusters are winding down; the fall TV line-up hasn't started. What's a Happy Woman to do to pass the time between work, prettifying, and men? Just kick off your heels, settle in your lawn chair with a frosty pitcher of margaritas and an SPF 15+ sunscreen, and check out these scintillating must-reads for fall!

The Book of Nosebleeds

By Vespasia Spivey

In this slim little volume, Vespasia Spivey packs a wealth of information on a poorly understood condition. Spivey dispels the myths surrounding the causes of nosebleeds (chickens, voodoo, poor moral character) and lists the true causes of epistaxis (picking, getting punched in the nose, evil spirits). A handy pullout guide offers step-by-step instructions on popular treatments (pinching your nose, pinching someone else's nose) and effective alternative therapies (corks, vices, leeches).

Spivey concludes with a fascinating glimpse into famous noses (Cyrano de Bergerac, Pinocchio, Rudolph the Red-Nosed Reindeer) and historical what-ifs. Did Elvis really die of a nosebleed? Was it chronic nosebleeds, and not her failure to produce a male heir, that sent Anne Boleyn to the chopping block?

Nights in White Satin: Folding Sheets and Other Domestic Adventures
By Maisey Kerfuffle

In this down-to-earth, yet philosophical addition to the "year-of" genre, Maisey Kerfuffle chronicles a year in her life as domestic goddess. Follow Maisey on her daily ritual of working like a galley slave to complete the meanest household chores while maintaining a cheery outlook and a drop-dead gorgeous figure. From making beds to cooking wholesome meals to waxing her kitchen appliances to the mysteries of folding fitted sheets, Maisey tells it all. Readers look on raptly as Maisey solves her clutter dilemmas, ponders life's meaning while ironing and watching daytime drama, and spring-cleans her fabulous makeup collection.

Pretzels and Clouds-Defining Their Inner Meaning
By Malva Malinga

The author examines the lifelong question of what the different shapes of broken pretzels and cirrus, stratus, and cumulus clouds portend. From the pretzel pince-nez we've all perched on our noses to the funnel cloud that left her with three broken limbs and a lacerated filtrum, Malinga deciphers it for us. Includes engaging detours into alphabet soup; Ouija boards; what it means when you get the black potato chip; and edible fashion advice (wearing Bugles as false fingernails).

Sojourns at Starbucks: Snooping in on Other People's Private Conversations
By Cotillion Carruthers

Fueled by DoubleShots™ and Espresso Macchiatos ("Espresso gently marked with foam"), the author takes us on a gleefully malicious tour of upscale coffee-shop chat. Includes dog fashions, laments on ugly flatware in restaurants, heated arguments over panini presses and what to put in perennial beds, man-snagging, how much to abase yourself to land a powerful client, and plenty of *braggadocio.*

Carruthers also provides a discerning evaluation of Starbucks coffees, from Arabian Mocha Java to Yukon Blend (her favorites are New Guinea Peaberry and Ethiopia Yergacheffe). She is currently undergoing rehabilitative treatment at the Greenspruce Centre for Caffeine Withdrawal in Montreal, paid for through stock-trading tips she picked up from overheard cell-phone exchanges.

Extreme Health Consumers
By Holly Buff

Follow the amazing feats and spectacularly ridiculous deaths of those who risk it all in pursuit of better health. The testosterone diet, which has 35 suddenly hirsute men carrying off women, swinging from cell-phone towers, and raiding the meat lockers at groceries. Read grotesque tales of vitamin mega-overdosers, with their veiny, bulging biceps, compound eyes, prehensile tails, and extra sets of legs (should they be allowed to compete in this year's Olympics?). Meet leather-skinned, crispy-fried women who've indulged their tanning-booth addictions to the max. Worst of all: the Extreme Makeover honeymoon that went horribly awry.

Cooking with Nettles
By Gerta Mandrake

Stinging nettles have taught many of us a vital lesson about nature-that it is a good thing to stay out of. Published in conjunction with Be Nice to Nettles Week in the UK, this book offers 100 eye-watering recipes for a much-maligned weed, including nettle bruschetta, nettle bisque, nettle-encrusted tuna with thinly julienned beets, Nettles Tatooine, nettle mousse, and nettle clusters.

Nettles are in fact extremely nutritious, a good source of calcium and magnesium that takes fibre to a whole new level. Excellent for nursing mothers since they cause increased milk production in cattle. Fed to horses to produce a sleek coat, nettles should be part of every woman's beauty regimen for smooth, luxurious skin. A nettle power bar, munched before an outdoors event, is better than bug spray at warding off flies.

For the more daring gourmand, Ms. Mandrake offers a special set of recipes cooked with a species of nettle from Timor that causes a burning sensation and lockjaw-like symptoms that may last weeks.* Her next two volumes: *Cooking with Poison Ivy and Poison Oak* and *Cooking with the Portuguese Man-of-War*. •*HW*•

**Nettle facts from www.nettles.org.uk.*

A Sexy Supermodel Shares her Secrets!

By Sharon Grehan

SUPERMODEL SUPREME Vim has graciously supplied all the tools you need to take you from yuck to yum! Follow her simple tips and you too could be sinsational!

Exercise:

I don't have time to work out in the traditional sense. My schedule is absolutely exhausting. I work one day every three weeks and that can run 10-12 hours, so rest is very important to me.

I keep hearing about the importance of exercise so I try to jiggle my foot while I'm watching television, doodle while I'm on the phone and shrug whenever I can.

Beauty Routine:

I usually get up in the morning and have a shower, especially when I'm working. I use soap because I find this keeps me clean and I dry off after with a towel. I like to brush my teeth with a toothbrush and I use deodorant faithfully.

Diet:

I have to watch what I eat because if I don't, I end up spilling. I usually remember to eat 2-3 times a day and I find mealtime is the best time to enjoy food.

	Day One	*Day Two*	*Day Three*
breakfast	4 cigarettes 6 cups black coffee	6 cigarettes 1 gallon Diet Coke	½ can cake frosting
lunch	1 pack Trident sugarless gum Diet Pepsi	3 glasses champagne 6 unsalted peanuts	n/a
dinner	½ bag Doritos Fat free pudding cup	Snickers bar	1 quart sugar-free iced tea and a cigar.

Final message: I wasn't always beautiful. There was a four day period in puberty where I was downright plain so I understand what some women are going through. Just remember like anything else in life that is worth having, it takes work and dedication. •*HW*•

Job Hunting:Dos and Don'ts
By Sharon Grehan

• *Don't* make repeated references to "the man."
• *Don't* ask for your résumé back as it is your only copy.
• *Don't* ask they if they check references before you provide them.
• *Don't* tell the interviewer you were fired from your last job because you were indispensable.
• *Do* show up on time for the interview; *don't* ask them how long it's going to take because you are so hung over you really need a nap.
• *Don't* call the interviewer "Cookie" or "Toots."
• *Don't* ask if they fire employees for stealing.
• *Do* tell them the reason for leaving your last job but *don't* tell them it was part of a conspiracy.
• *Don't* ask the interviewer if there are any "babes" working there.
• *Don't* try to skirt answers, for example: if you are asked if you have ever been charged with sexual harassment *don't* say "it depends on what you mean by sexual harassment."
• *Don't* tell the interviewer when you are asked what your goals are, that you would like to have a job like theirs because it is so easy.
• *Don't* ask them at the interview if it is possible to get an advance on your wages.
• When they ask you what type of job you are seeking don't ask them to guess.

HW DISPATCH:

Mother who Forgot to Call Olly-Olly-Oxen-Free Jailed for Child Abuse

"Well, it was my turn to be 'it' in a game of hide-and-seek," said Jane Junedoll, "and I counted to ten, the kids scattered, and then I went in the living room and sat down to enjoy an hour of peace and quiet watching *Oprah*. One thing led to another, and the next thing I know it's Saturday and the kids are still 'hiding.'"—*E. Hanes.*

Supermodel To Resume Eating

At a hastily called press conference today, Italian supermodel Vivendi Universal announced her retirement. "Now that my best modelling years are behind me, I plan to eat like a pig," the 24-year-old said.

"It's been a great ride, and I don't regret the starvation, the self-deprivation or the frequent hospital stays for intravenous fluid therapy," she added. "However, I'm relieved I can now stuff myself and retire as a fat old woman."

Smiling for the paparazzi (who had all been ordered to stand to the left in order to photograph Universal's "good" side), the former supermodel ushered in her retirement by pigging out on a strand of pasta and four kernels of corn. —*E. Hanes.*

The Rules of Family: Advice from Donna Corleone

By Pamela Monk

DEAR MADRONE,
I am a teacher in a big university in a state that I will not name, for fear that the big shots up top will not take kindly to my complaint. Keep it in the family they say, only they are not my family, *capish?* Anyway, in two different classes in the past week, the cell phone rings and a boy jumps up saying to me, I have to take this call, it's my mother. Can you believe it? What can I do to put an end to this? I am prevented, by state law, from wringing their necks.
Anonymous from Anywhere

Dear AFA
What are you, cracked? You're going to tell a boy not to talk to his mother? And what if he listens to you? That's worse. Two possibilities—mamma is phoning in with the results of major surgery or something like it, so what can you do? Or two, she is just making sure the apron strings are pulled tight around the *testicolos,* in which case, there is nothing you can do either. Of course, it also might be that they just SAY it's their mother so you can not interrupt, this is on their heads, and the time and place of their pay back is not up to you. Just know that it will come.
God bless, Donna

Chapter Nine – September

Supermodels Pick the Right Religion For You!

By Sharon Grehan

"Every religion emphasizes human improvement, love, respect for others, sharing other people's suffering. On these lines every religion had more or less the same viewpoint and the same goal."
—The Dalai Lama

THE FASHION HOUSES have spoken. Pink is in, as are kicky purses, but what's the buzz in the houses of the holy? We have chosen six of today's hottest supermodels to find out what's setting the holy circles ablaze!

Anna Moizen is originally from Athens, Georgia. She is 6' even and weighs 98 pounds. She is renowned for her saucy stroll and for having the most versatile nose.

"I think religion is a great way to get world peace."

Anna chose:

Roman Catholic Church

- Catholics believe in prayer, limbo and purgatory and that hell is a state of being.
- They believe that the original writings by Bible authors are inerrant.
- Confession is thought to provide forgiveness.
- Debate is sometimes forbidden.
- They worship statues of God, Jesus, Mary and all the saints.

Anna: I love *The Sopranos* and Veal Marsala, so this was a natural choice for me. The confession part is good so you don't have anything hanging over your head just in case. Forbidding debate is also good in that you only have to learn things once.

The Downside: The statues are very tacky and the women don't age well.

Ilize Fulcrom: Originally from Wisconsin, Ilize has been blazing a runway trail for over 2½ months. At 6' 1" and 102 pounds with cheekbones you could hang your hat on, Ilize says:

"I think religion is really important to keep you holy."

Ilize chose:

Buddhism

- Buddhists don't believe in the one supreme God nor do they believe in prayer, heaven or hell.
- They do believe in reincarnation and meditation and encourage detachment from desire and the self.

Ilize: I picked this because it is the hottest religion out there. It is sufficiently mysterious that you could probably get days off work for religious holidays and you can make up whatever you want to win a debate with non-Buddhists.

I like the idea of meditating too, because that's something I can do while I'm working instead of humming.

The Downside: The reincarnation aspect. Since I'm wealthy, attractive and happy in this life, I'm kinda scared of coming back next time as a leper or even worse, fat.

I hope that detachment from desire

and the self doesn't mean no makeup. If it does, I'll go the Catholic route.

Magra Doucet: Magra, from Sault Ste. Marie Ontario (*ooh la la!* it sounds exotic!) At 5' 11" and 98 pounds, Magra's nine yard legs have been a shutterbug's dream.

"I think religion is a good thing to have if you don't have luck."

Magra chose:

United Church of Christ

- These Christians believe that Satan is only a symbol and does not exist and that hell is either a temporary punishment or a symbolic one.
- They interpret the Bible in many ways. They feel some passages are symbolic, some literal and they believe that some passages should be ignored.
- They do not believe the end of the world is imminent, and the requirements for joining are minimal.

Magra: I was really drawn to this religion because it seems to require the least effort—I travel a lot and don't have a lot of time.

Their hell is only temporary, like tight shoes, and ignoring passages of the Bible makes sense because I've heard it's really loooong.

The Downside: It might involve casseroles.

Billy Wild, originally from London England has been gracing covers all over the world. At 6"2 and 108 pounds, Billy has been called one of the most beautiful women alive.

"Religion is very much like exercise in that I think it is the key to finding your inner peace and spirituality.

I've thought many times of giving up exercise and just concentrating on religion but unfortunately you don't lose a lot of weight with religion."

Billy chose:

Southern Baptist Convention

- They believe that Satan exists and is profoundly powerful and that not only does hell exist, it's worse than we thought.
- They interpret the Bible literally.
- They have a "Prime Directive" and that is to evangelize the word.
- They believe that converting Jews to Christianity is of utmost importance and that the end of the world is near.

Billy: I liked this religion because I've seen *Gone With The Wind* about 10 times. I have a passion for mint juleps, alligators, wood—anything that's from the south!

This religion is perfect for anyone who likes hard and fast rules like I do and approaching complete strangers on the bus.

The Downside: At first I was put off because of big hair but then I found out it's coming back so I was relieved. The only bummer is their world is going to end sooner than the others but then again it is kind of like modelling.

Betsy Richards is a petite beauty from Illinois. Standing at a mere 5' 8' and 81

> *"...unfortunately you don't lose a lot of weight with religion."*

pounds, her success has astounded many fashion critics.

"Because of my height I believe it was religion that placed me at the top. Every time I would go to an audition I would hold my crystal, cross my fingers and pray. It has really paid off."

Betsy's choice:

Judaism

(We will leave out the "o" in G-d to respect the Jewish prohibition against spelling the name in full.)

- They believe G-d is the creator of all that exists.
- They believe He rewards good behaviour and punishes bad behaviour.
- Beliefs about Jesus vary. He is considered a false prophet by some and a teacher by others.

Betsy: Their G-d is almost like the Tommy Hilfiger of g-ds so you know who to worship without getting mixed up.

They also have great comedians. I like the idea of rewarding good behaviour and punishing bad behaviour; that seems to be fair and would probably make somebody think twice of putting glue in your face spritz.

The Downside: The food looks really fattening and the religion sounds a little time-consuming, also the idea of leaving vowels out of words may catch on, like it's hard enough to read stuff now, so I don't like that.

Vim. This one-named wonder is setting the modelling world on its ear. She started modelling at the age of 14 and feels that coming into this profession at such a late age has made this sultry 5' 10" 94 pound beauty a little more introspective.

"As far as religion goes, I'm really for it. I'm against hunger and the environment and everything but really for religion."

Her religion of choice was:

Islam

- They believe that God is the creator and have great respect for earlier prophets and they believe in their teachings.
- They believe that Muslims who repent will enter Paradise and that sinners and unbelievers will burn for all eternity in Hell.
- Abstinence from alcohol, drugs, pork and gambling is required.
- They regard the Christian concept of Jesus as deity to be blasphemous.

Vim: Chadors are terrific for hiding thick ankles and chubby thighs, and Paradise sounds kind of like Capri.

The Downside: I think I would have enjoyed it more if I had joined 1400 years ago, and I really enjoy a hot-dog when I'm not working. •*HW*•

Herstory: Finding Your Spirit!
Our Readers Share Their Secrets!
By Sharon Grehan

I LIKE TO WATCH reruns of inspirational TV shows like *Little House on the Prairie, The Waltons* or *Saved by the Bell.* After the program is over I draw pictures of the characters on felt, cut them out, act out the most poignant scenes then watch myself cry in the mirror. —*Mrs. Michael Levine, Montana*

About once a month or so I gather the children together just before dinner, I announce to them that their Daddy was in a terrible accident and isn't coming home anymore. I wait until their grief is spent and then tell them I'm joking. We then discuss how horrible it would be if it were true. It brings us closer together as a family. —*Mrs. Francine Pet*

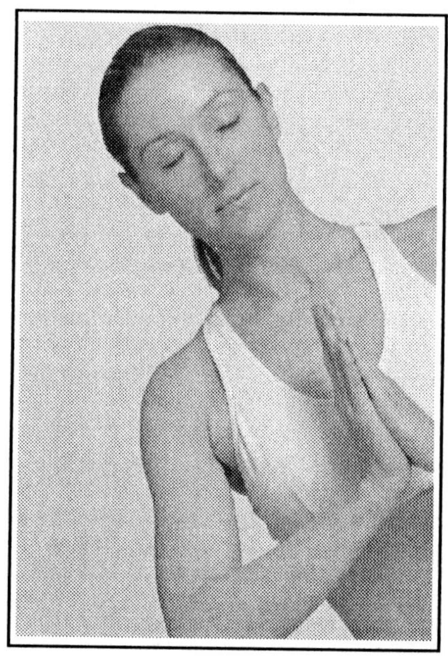

Whenever I am waiting for a bus, I hold my breath until I start to lose consciousness. It is the only way I can come close to experiencing dying, thus enhancing the living experience. It also makes good use of down time. —*Meg Brazil*

"I count my blessings every day at 4 p.m. out loud on the subway..."

I drive my children to a very poor part of town so we can look at the underprivileged people. We throw cans of food out of the window and then go for ice cream. —*D. Parkston*

I count my blessings every day at 4 p.m. out loud on the subway. I really feel I'm setting a good example for the other passengers. After I finish counting my blessings I start reading aloud from my Maledict List just so people don't think I'm a Jesus freak. —*Edith Perzan*

The Loneliest Barstool
By Sarah W. Szucs

ALTHOUGH GETTING TO singlehood may have been a painful and tear-filled event, you're here now. Welcome to the club!

Let's start with a few quick tips for all newcomers getting into the pool. First off, look in the mirror. Was it your fault your last mate left? Is your hair limp? Is your face too puffy? Immediately start dieting and get a perm. Also, now is the time to experiment with makeup—your face is a canvas and Cupid awaits! Lastly, go through your closet and throw out everything that doesn't make you look hot. You've got to market yourself and there's a lot of competition to deal with.

Now, on to the party! Being single means saying "yes" to any and every social invitation that drifts your way, and finagling your way into invitations that somehow circumvented your mailbox. Make friends with all the single people you know, and go out with them whenever you are not at work. This will give you someone to talk to while hunting Mr. Right, and keep you from smelling of complete desperation.

Many singles enjoy being out in public, mingling with other single-minded people. Going out after work to happy hour is a major step in establishing your singlehood status. Meeting new people, trying new drinks and eating free hors d' oeuvres is quite conducive to the formation of new and exciting romance.

Single people like having fun, and after a few two-for-one drink specials, dancing is a big part of that fun. Once you are on the dance floor, be sure to stand in a circle with all of your single friends. You are prime real estate and want to be seen by the entire bar. Proper "product placement" is a key factor in catching the eye of Mr. Right.

The dance steps for the single woman on the prowl should show off her best qualities. If you have beautiful, dreamy eyes make sure to do lots of hand gesturing that show them off. Some of these movements may be dramatic fanning of the hands around the head, or playful peek-a-boo motions towards anyone gazing at you. Should you have lovely nails, the same movements may be done, but be sure to emphasize the fact that your ring finger is barren. This green light will let Mr. Right know that yes, you are indeed available.

Some women have an interest in showing off other physical attributes. To draw attention to your torso, backside or clapping ability you need to have an engaging dance that will both entertain and entrance potential mates. This simple dance is most effective when performed in a circle with your other single friends. With the left foot leading take one step forward. Bring the right foot forward up next to the left foot, touchdown, then quickly swing the right foot out to the right side about twelve inches. Next, bring the left foot over twelve inches to meet the right foot.

Touch down with the left foot then quickly bring the left foot backwards twelve inches. The right foot at that point should swing back twelve inches to meet the left foot. The left foot should quickly be brought over twelve inches to the left. With your weight bearing down on the left foot, bring the right foot over twelve inches to the left and touchdown.

Repeat this "square step" dance in time to the music, while clapping enthusiastically with every foot movement. (Note: the dance ends when the music stops. Be sure to adjust the tempo of your dance to the various rhythms playing throughout the evening. This dance may be done while chatting with other dancers and looks good to have a drink in one hand, except if clapping. Purses may be piled in the centre of the dancing square steppers for safekeeping.)

Once a potential suitor approaches you it is easy for him to join in on the fun of the circle of square steppers. You may talk with him lightheartedly in an atmosphere of circle safety. As songs are short, get down to the basics as soon as you establish eye contact. Suggestions for things to find out in two minutes or less: religious beliefs, baggage, plans for the future, income, and if he is wearing a wedding ring find out if he is really serious about his wife.

Be warned, as long as you remain in the circle of square steppers you will continue be joined by other potential mates. Remember to have fun and not take things too seriously. This is your time to enjoy life and bask in the knowledge that the more mates you seduce into joining the square stepping circle the greater your chance of getting to the altar by next Valentines Day! •*HW*•

Do it Yourself Projects: Human Cloning Designer Genes!

By Sharon Grehan

WHAT A WONDERFUL age we live in! Years ago, having children was rather messy and more than a little risky. Mixing your weak chin with his family's anteater proboscis was a gamble at best, and for ages moms-to-be fretted nights away wondering, "What will my baby look like?" Well fret no more, mommy!

A big fat kiss on the lips to modern science for coming up with this eye-saver: human cloning!

What to do first:

- Ovulate.
- Scout out shopping malls or bars and gyms for very good looking people.
- When you see the perfect specimen, go up very close and scratch them. The arm is good but the inside of the mouth is perfect—it's just harder to do without them noticing.
- Preserve the tissue under your fingernails.
- Remove your unfertilized egg and remove all genetic material. Tip: It is best to do this at home and not at the mall. (You may also need a magnifying glass and a lab.)

• Remove the nucleus from the good-looking donor's cell and place it next to the egg.

• Force a tiny spark of electricity across the two by scuffing your feet repeatedly on a nylon carpet. The two cells will then fuse.

• Once the fertilized egg grows to 50 to 100 cells, implant the embryo in a woman's womb. (You, or perhaps your housekeeper, but it is just plain courteous to tell the person in advance.)

The egg thinks it's been fertilized, it gets a full set of genes, divides and becomes an identical twin!! That's all there is to it! Wasn't that fun? •*HW*•

Note: There has been some concern that when cloning, the chromosomes could match the age of the donor. For example a 10 year old would look like a 20 year old and a 20 year old would look like a 40 year old. As a result, the potential for cancer and heart disease will increase. If that does happen, it's probably best just to use the bundle of joy for parts!

How to Make Your Child a Star!!!!

By Sharon Grehan

SUSAN WENTWORTH GENTLY dries her daughter's tears. "Sangria, we talked about this, what did we say?"

Sangria takes a brave sniff and raises her trembling chin "You said if I ate like a little piggy no one would love me and I would never get to be on TV."

Satisfied, Susan smiles and hands a fat free Nutribar to Sangria. She takes Sangria's hand and they leave the casting agent's office humbled by rejection.

"It's harder than it looks," admits casting agent Jenn Whitney-Macran-Hallow-Bowes "Not only does the child have to have a certain *oomph* quality, he or she has to be intelligent, attractive, or if not attractive, at least ugly in an interesting way, and it does not hurt to have talent."

Sound discouraging? Well statistically, the chances of your child being a major television star are a million to one, but there are many, many avenues for ambitious mothers to explore. If all you're looking for is second-hand gratification and a way for your child to earn money, acting may be just the way to go.

Getting Started

Photos and Representation: Have your child's photos taken by a professional photographer, if you don't know of a reputable photographer then check the classifieds of any big city daily. Look under the sections that start with "Earn Big Money Acting in Commercials." If your child meets the criteria that Jenn Whitney-Macran-Hallow-Bowes stated above and you have $5,000, you are well on the road to stardom.

Pursue leads on your own. Don't just wait for your agent to do all the work, you have to do some legwork on your own. Enroll your child in beauty pageants, enter them in any contest that requires a photo, and offer free modelling services.

A little known fact is that casting agents are known to roam malls in search of talent, so hang around the entrance to major department stores. Dressing your child up in theme clothing is a guaranteed attention getter for example: a pilgrim for Thanksgiving, a football for Superbowl. You are only limited by your imagination and by how much weight your child can carry on their head.

The Circus is often overlooked, but opportunities for travel abound.

Be aware that this is a full time job. No child ever made it to a classic like *Full House* by eating Twinkies and rotting away in a classroom. If you are diligent, you will be rewarded with more money than you ever dreamed and a precocious little moppet that anyone would be proud of!

Tips

- Your child must be very, very slim or very, very fat. There is no in-between. "Little fat children can be very humorous," says an industry insider "but there is not as much work once they get older and become hard to look at."
- A gimmick goes a long way. Teach your child an interesting talent like yodelling or line dancing.

The must have: An impish grin is a big seller. Even jaded professionals melt in the presence of a child with a carefully prepared smile.

- To do so: Have your child stand in front of the mirror and smile naturally.
- Carefully examine his/her face for flaws. Keep in mind that pudgy cheeks and missing teeth are 'gimmes' and not flaws.
- Have the child smile as wide as they possibly can. They won't be able to hold the position long at first, but with practice they will be able to maintain the grin for up to three hours.
- Once the smile is set in place have them crinkle their eyes so that the nose becomes upturned.

A simple tip of the head with hands clasped in front and *voila!* •*HW*•

Sidestepping the Coogan Law

This law requires that 15 percent of a child's earnings be put in trust until the child turns 18, but luckily the law doesn't extend to the 37 states without child labour laws, so you may consider moving. Acting as your child's manager will increase your earnings and there is a wide interpretation of "due diligence" in handling finances. As well, it is not unethical to charge a child of 8 room and board. This is fair and even common in many countries around the world.

The Balanced Diet – Guaranteed to Work!

By Sharon Grehan

IT IS WELL KNOWN that the way to healthy weight loss is through sensible dieting and exercise. With this program you will be burning every calorie you consume (and then some!) By giving you two exercise options it is tailor-made to fit every lifestyle.

In only one month and with just a little effort, you can go from a flabby Frieda to a fit Francie!

Day One

Breakfast

- 100-Percent Bran Cereal in 2-Percent Milk - 137 Calories
- Whole-wheat Bread Slice - 70 calories
- Butter Pat - 36 calories
- Peach - 37 calories
- Coffee-6 oz. - 4 calories

Total: 284 calories

The Burn Off: Two hours canoeing or one hour of cricket.

Lunch

- 2 oz. Roast Beef and 1 oz. Swiss on White - 339 calories
- Small Green Salad-1.5 cups - 33 calories
- Diet French Dressing-4 tbsp - 83 calories
- Orange - 62 calories
- Skim Milk-8 oz. - 86 calories

Total: 603 calories

The Burn Off: One hour rock climbing or three hours fishing.

Dinner

- Roast Turkey-6 oz. - 355 calories
- Cooked Brown Rice-1 cup- 216 calories
- Brussel Sprouts-1 cup - 61 calories
- Strawberries-1 cup - 45 calories a
- Water-8 oz. contains 0 calories
- Lowfat Fruit Yogurt-8 oz.-231 calories

Total: 908 calories

The Burn Off: Six hours horseback riding or three hours snowmobiling.

Day Two

Breakfast

- 1 hard-boiled egg - 93 calories
- 1 bagel - 195 calories
- 1 pat butter - 36 calories
- 6 oz cup black coffee 4 calories

Total: 328 calories and 11.57 grams of fat.

The Burn Off: One hour fencing or five hours licking stamps.

Lunch

- Large Green Salad-3 cups - 66 calories
- Diet Italian Dressing-4 tbsp. - 63 calories
- Seedless Raisins-1 cup - 435 calories Stalk of Raw Celery - 6 calories
- Water-8 oz. - 0 calories

Total: 570 calories

The Burn Off: 1½ hours dolphin training or four hours showering.

Dinner

- 6 oz. Spaghetti with 1 oz. Marinara Sauce - 325 calories
- Small Tossed Salad-1 ½ cups - 33

calories

• Mixed Vegetables-1 cup - 107 calories
Fruit Cocktail in Juice-1 cup - 114 calories

• Skim Milk-8 oz. - 86 calories

Total: 665 calories and 6.20 grams of fat

The Burn Off: One hour roofing or four hours of croquet.

Day Three

Breakfast

• Scrambled Egg - 100 calories
• Whole Wheat Pita - 170 calories
• Margarine-1 tsp.- 34 calories
• Apple - 81 calories
• Coffee-6 oz. - 4 calories

Total: 389 calories

The Burn Off: One Hour sawing wood or 1 ½ hours piloting a riverboat.

Lunch

• Chicken Vegetable Soup-19 oz. - 372 calories
• White Bread Slice - 67 calories
• Margarine-1 tsp.. - 34 calories
• Pear - 98 calories a
• Water-8 oz. - 0 calories

Total: 571 calories

The Burn Off: One hour pro football or nine hours babysitting.

Dinner

• Roast Chicken Breast-6 oz. - 284 calories
• Baked Potato - 220 calories
• Asparagus-1 cup - 43 calories
• Grapes-1 cup - 58 calories
• Skim Milk-8 oz. - 86 calories
• Vanilla Frozen Yogurt-1 cup - 229 calories

Total: 920 calories

The Burn Off: One hour firefighting or eleven hours archery.

Follow this diet for two weeks or the rest of your life and watch as those *how-do's* turn into *hubba-hubbas!* •*HW*•

The Goldilocks Syndrome: Getting Rid of the Bears in Your Life
By Elaine Langlois

Are there situations in your life that are simply too hot? Do you feel left out in the cold? Do you find it impossible to get to a place that feels just right?

A hot new best-seller offers us answers for these and other modern dilemmas: The *Goldilocks Syndrome: Getting Rid of the Bears in Your Life. The Goldilocks Syndrome* is the latest work of popular psychologist Verdetta Dervish, whose previous books include *Letting Your Hair Down with Rapunzel* and *Negotiating to Win: Lessons from The Three Billy Goats Gruff.*

"It's no accident that fairy tales have endured in Western civilization for so many years," Dervish tells us. "Fairy tales are a source of fundamental wisdom that, with insight, can be applied to our personal and professional lives."

We all know the Goldilocks story. A little girl, wandering in a forest, comes upon a deserted house. She tastes porridge that is too hot and some that is too cold before devouring a bowl that's "just right." She sits in a chair that's too small (breaking it) and one that's too large before finding one that's "just right." She tries a too-soft bed and a too-hard bed before finding one that's-you guessed it- "just right." She falls asleep. The householders, who happen to be bears, return, waking Goldilocks, who is frightened and runs away.

So what lessons can we draw from this tale? Here's what *The Goldilocks Syndrome* has to say:

Find the golden mean. Sophrosyne, the Greeks called it. Get a boat. Steer a middle course. Avoid the highs and lows. Take Dramamine if you need it. Practice moderation and restraint. Look for whales. You could do some wakeboarding, too.

Rediscover the little girl in you. Take a walk in the woods. Leave your cell phone and pager at home (but make a trail for yourself with breadcrumbs). Bring a basket of food to your grandmother. Play with your old paper dolls and Barbies.

Be choosy. Take the time and effort to find what's "just right" for you. This applies to food, furniture, jobs, and mammals!

Organize. Now that you know what you do want, get rid of everything you don't. Organize your life from top to bottom. Throw out that broken chair and everything else you haven't used in the past two years. Strip your life to the bear necessities. The bear essentials. Buy a planner. Write in the planner. Don't lose the planner.

Explore the health benefits of porridge. Once

"Fairy tales are a source of fundamental wisdom..."

eaten only by mischievous urchins in fairy tales and indigent orphans in novels like *Jane Eyre*, porridge is the wonder food of the 21st century. It lowers cholesterol, clears up sinus infections, and has natural weight-reduction properties. Applied to the skin, it's an effective exfoliant and an excellent remedy for acne.

Get rid of the bears in your life. This is *The Goldilocks Syndrome*'s most important lesson. Face up to your bears. See them for what they are. Understand why you are in this destructive relationship with them. Now you are ready to make a creative plan for overcoming your bears. Call pest control. Make smelly rugs out of them.

Get in touch with your inner bear. At this point, you can move forward to internalize the positive aspects of being a bear. Adapt to your environment. Don't let anyone invade your territory. Learn the effectiveness of a well-placed growl or powerful forepaw strike. Expand your diet to include acorns, honey, bees, garbage, rodents, termites, and grubs. Climb trees. Fix up a cozy den. Mate frequently. Take really long naps.

Don't feed the bears. How many times do we have to tell you? Feeding just encourages them.

Like the song says, "Fairy tales can come true. It can happen to you." Deal with your bears and you can change your life. It may be difficult but, at the end of it all, you could find yourself in a castle with lots of nice clothes and furniture, a terrific car, expensive jewelry, and lots of other portable property, with Mr. Just Right. •*HW*•

HW DISPATCH: News for Happy Women

Woman Fails to Sell Newspaper Collection at Auction, Sues eBay
A Minot, ND, housewife has sued online auctioneer eBay over her failed bid to sell her newspaper collection. "I get the daily paper, and what are you supposed to do after you're done reading it? I stack mine up in the corner, but the pile had nearly reached the ceiling. I thought, 'Maybe I could make a few extra dollars by selling these on eBay.' So, I listed them but didn't get a single bid. I want my listing fees back, but eBay says no." Shockingly, not a single bidder showed any interest in the collection of 148 issues of the Minot Record-Reporter, dated between March and July, 2002. eBay's attorneys had no comment. —*E. Hanes*

Satan Sues 43,000,000 for Copyright Infringement

Claiming he invented Deviled Eggs on the eighth day, the Prince of Darkness has launched a class action lawsuit against kitchen economists across the nation. "I first invented the hard cooked eggs with tangy filling as a vehicle for tempting Eve, but the apple turned out to be a better option, since it didn't require refrigeration," Satan said. "I immediately set down detailed instructions on how to make them because I knew they would be a real hit at potlucks." Indeed, the rubbery half-eggs have proven to be a summer picnic and holiday staple. Various recipes for Deviled Eggs have appeared in cookbooks over the years, and Satan argues he holds copyright to all of those various incarnations. Copyright attorney Lance Fulbright doubts the devil will be able to prevail in his lawsuit. "I have two words for Mr. Prince of Darkness: public domain," said Fulbright. However, Satan claims he's still alive and well—pointing to the Iraq War and Michael Jackson as recent examples of his handiwork—and believes he will win his case.

—E.Hanes

The Rules of Family: Advice from Donna Corleone

By Pamela Monk

DEAR MADRONE,

I drive my cousin to the station every day on my way to work, he never offers gas money. Is not this freeloading, should I not demand what is rightfully my share? My mother says to forget it, her sister is the same way, but I do not have a gracious heart about this.

Doormat, Stony Brook

Dear Mat,

If you ask for the money directly, be prepared for your mother to berate you and your aunt and your cousin to talk against you. But now, in the favour bank, he has opened an account in your name. It is good for one big request, or many little ones, all depending upon how long you've been dropping him off, and how far you must go out of your way to do so. If he refuses what you ask, then he is the *shem*, not you. Sometimes I am amazed at the things I must spell out.

God bless, Donna

Chapter Ten – October

Halloween Safety: Tips to Keep Our Children Safe

By Sharon Grehan

Costumes

IT IS ABSOLUTELY necessary to keep your children warm. Start with sections of newspaper taped to the chest, over this put a pair of long johns and a woolen vest. Add a cardigan and an extra pair of pants. Finish off with their winter coat, two pairs of socks and mitts. To make sure your child is visible at all times, reflective tape striped over the costume is effective, as is a miner's helmet.

You might have to let the costume out to accommodate the extra layers of clothing. 6-8 inch strips of corduroy or heavy fleece would do the job nicely.

Test the flame retardancy of his or her costume by setting fire to an inconspicuous spot. If the costume bursts into flame then you might want to pick up another. It is probably best to do these tests when your child is not wearing the costume. As an added precaution, a few middle of the night "Stop-Drop-Roll" emergency drills certainly wouldn't hurt.

Some masks impair vision. To make sure your child has a good sightline, put the costume on the child, spin, him or her 10 times (the estimated amount of turns the average child will make in one evening. If your child is a dancer or lopsided they may turn more.) Then ask them to retrieve an object at the end of your driveway. If your child slams into your garage door or worse, takes a header halfway up the driveway then there is a good chance the mask will shift during the festivities. Either replace the mask or use spirit gum and glue it to the child's head. The strength of the glue can be gauged by whether or not you want Spiderman in your Christmas photos.

Consider modern day villains that don't require masks and in some cases only require a simple blue shirt. For example, a Parking Authority Officer, Enron Executive, or Martha Stewart.

Trick or Treating

A minimum of two parents is necessary. There are probably millions of cases where a parent sneezed or paused to wipe a bead of sweat and their child was never, ever, ever, *ever* seen again. If both parents are not available that evening consider hiring off duty police officers.

A global positioning satellite (GPS) is a must-have for the conscientious parent. The device will display the child's location, speed, heading, lat/lon and time at remote location. One word of warning: signals cannot go through metal so make sure your child is not going as a robot.

A cell phone is also a must-have. Program 911 into the telephone. Do a few tests with a stopwatch and keep an eye on the response time.

Children must avoid dimly lit houses at all costs and be on the alert for inappropriate behaviour and suspicious strangers. For example, have your children steer clear of cackling bearded wild-eyed men with bad teeth who ask children if they want to make a quick sawbuck.

At each new house check around the property for flower pots, low tree limbs, support wires, uneven mounds of grass, loose pebbles, stray leaves or garden hoses that may prove hazardous.

Tiny tootsies will tire quite rapidly so you may wish to soften the tread by purchasing a 10-12 foot runner carpet from your local hardware store. Simply roll the carpet out as your child makes his/her progress. Be sure to sweep the street first as dirt and germs could easily adhere to the fibres.

Children should also be reassured at frequent intervals. After every house hug your child fiercely and whisper that you will always love them *no matter what!*

Candy

At your own home you can break the chain of tooth decay by offering healthy snacks. Tofu rolled in a granola, steamed veggies or how about making the evening truly special by writing a song? The gift of music is always appreciated.

If inconsiderate parents insist on giving out sweets, coach your child to say "Thank you but I'd prefer some yogurt or cheese" (if your child is lactose intolerant they may add cash to this request.)

If you were unable to stem the candy flow then once home you might slip Grandpa's dentures or Auntie's partial plate into the goody bag.

Halloween Parties

Bobbing for apples, a very popular Halloween party game, is to be avoided. Not only for the obvious drowning hazard but for the competitive spirit it encourages. Better to hand each child an apple and praise them for being special and different.

If you are planning a party, best to eliminate most traditional games because they send terrible messages to the child. "Pin the Tail on the Donkey" is a good example of this but other less brutal games still pose risk. "Statues" restricts child's freedom of expression, "Kick the Can" may change their mind about recycling—the list goes on and on.

Work with your children to come up with alternatives. The "I Like You Because..." game will provide hours of raucous fun as will "I Have an Apple, Would You Like One Too?"

With these tips in mind we hope you have a healthy, if not happy, Halloween! •*HW*•

Celine Dion Pumpkin Stencil

By Sharon Grehan

WHAT YOUNGSTER WOULDN'T appreciate a toothsome treat from a house that featured this long-chinned lovely?

Pumpkin Carving Tools

- large spoon
- sharp knife
- nail
- paring knife

Carving Your Pumpkin

1. Cut out the stencil. If you have a very large pumpkin you might want to copy and enlarge the drawing. If you have a very tiny pumpkin you might want to reduce the size of the drawing. If you don't have a pumpkin, you don't need a pumpkin stencil, you need a pumpkin.
2. Tape the stencil to your pumpkin (sticky side down)

Celine Stencil

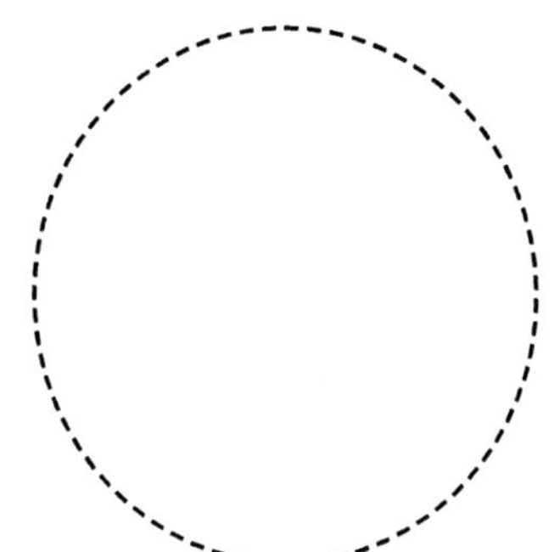

3. Using the nail (sharp side down) punch holes through the paper, into the pumpkin, following the lines of the stencil. Be careful not to put your finger directly behind the holes and do not use a hammer.
4. Use the sharp knife to cut a circle at the top of the pumpkin. (Circle stencil above.)
5. Scoop out the insides. You might want to sing one of Celine's hit songs at this point. Recommended: *I Drove All Night.* (Hint: changing the word "drove" to "dug" is a hilarious thing to do.)
6. Scrape the insides with the large spoon (Hint: the spoon should be large enough to make light work but small enough to fit inside the top of the pumpkin. If you have to bash the spoon repeatedly against the opening the spoon might be too big.)
7. Use the paring knife to cut along the dotted lines you have made with the nail. You should cut them in order.
8. Cut a hole to be used as a vent in the top of the pumpkin, shove a candle inside Celine's head and Voila! •*HW*•

Beauty 911

By Elize Bergeron

Q: I AM IN LOVE WITH Manolo Blahnik shoes. The only problem is I can't seem to walk or stand in them. I have very broad feet and the tapered toes make mobility a near impossibility. What should I do?

A: First of all, your very broad feet concern me. Feet (like the derrière) spread with constant use. But let's assume you are an Olympian not a poseur: I feel your main problem is prioritizing. You must ask yourself one of the most important questions of your life.

What do you want out of footwear?

If you wish to shout to the world "Look! I spent $637.00 on a pair of shoes that are impossible to walk in because I have loads of money and am therefore better than you." then your standing and walking problems are easily solved with two words: Taxi. Chair.

If however, comfort is your primary concern, then not only are you doing Manolo a disservice you are ruining it for women who *can* wear this fabulous footwear. I suggest you invest in a pair of Tender Tootsies and head off to bingo.

Fashion is power. And with power comes responsibility. Fashion, in the wrong hands, breaks down carefully drawn lines of class-distinction. Please remember that.

It is ultimately your decision, but this is a matter that needs careful consideration.

Perhaps you could talk to your minister.

Q: I just found out that big shoulders are coming back in style. I am devastated as I spent a considerable sum on jackets last season. I don't feel I can afford to replace them. Elize, instead of investing in new jackets, couldn't I just put in some shoulder pads?

A: No.

Cut Out for Halloween: The Carve Craze™

By Christina Delia

By now, most cautious calorie counters have found ample reason to rule out carbs, meat, and dairy. It seems that the only foods allowed to appear at mealtime are fruits and veggies, yet many women remain unhappy with their figures. Luckily, you can now rule out fruit and veggies, too! This fall, women will be putting their faith in The Carve Diet™, and as a result, putting on the happy faces (and taking off the pounds!)

Carve *is a seasonal diet*

The Carve Diet™ is designed to fit in ideally during the weeks before Halloween rears its ugly, store-bought-mask-covered head. With The Carve Diet™, you will still enjoy regular doses of fruit and vegetables, but in smaller, *Carve*-friendly, portions.

Here's where the happy faces come in

The most delightful part of The Carve Craze™ is that it is as easy to follow as purchasing and carving a store-bought pumpkin. All one needs to do is obtain the usual assortment of fruits and vegetables, and then take them home for carving (just like you would *Carve* a pumpkin into a jack-o-lantern!) Voila! Can you say eyes, nose, and mouth? Then you've just *Carved* yourself a winning, grinning dinner! *Carve*-Conscious Clue: Feed those apple and onion leftovers to Carve-Clueless boyfriends, husbands, and pets.

It's easy to train your brain to Carve! Here are some helpful hints to get you started:

- *Carve* only what is fit for carving
- *Carve*-friendly foods include apples, tomatoes, and melons. Basically, anything you can *Carve* a face onto without it falling apart. This will cut down on snacking temptation, by initially eliminating non-*Carve*-worthy vegetables and fruits from your diet. Orange you glad you didn't eat that banana?
- *Carve* is your new best friend . Unlike your girlfriends and coworkers who will occasionally spot you a baked potato, *Carve* really does want you to look great. Before you eat your meals, look at your plate. That little fruit or vegetable face is not solely there to be consumed. It should be looked upon as a source of guidance and motivation, not just nutrients.

Yet woman can not live on *Carve* alone

The Carve Diet™, (much like cheap plastic fangs that break off in your mouth), screams of Halloween. Oh sure, you might be tempted to *Carve* during the long winter months or the slow summer season, but be sure to incorporate *Carve* into your regularly scheduled eating program. A little *Carve* now and then is harmless, but if *Carve* has become something that you Crave, it might be time to take that triangularly shaped green pepper nose out of your mouth...until next Halloween. •*HW*•

A Stress Free Thanksgiving!!!

By Sharon Grehan

AS THE NAME suggests, Thanksgiving should be a time of giving thanks. A time to appreciate what we have and who we have to share with. It is also a time where a fully grown woman can be scorned and marginalized for putting on a few pounds while her sister, the high-school dropout is praised to high heaven for teaching her slack-jawed son to say "paw paw."

If your family portrait would be better represented by Arbus than Rockwell these tips are for you!

Stay Calm

The first mistake people make is to let emotion take over. If a comment is addressed to you, before you take offense ask yourself this, "Is the person really saying this to be hurtful?" If the answer is no, just let it go. If you are unsure, discuss the issue at a later time one to one.

For example at a dinner hosted by Sister A, Sister B asks "How is your career going?" Sister A knows that there are quotes around "career." She knows that Sister B is getting in a dig. She knows that Sister B is saying, "Look at me, I married rich and here you are flailing around like a beached halibut."

Sister A feels that even if she does have to write stupid self-help articles for a two-bit nickel and dime woman's magazine that doesn't come close to covering the bills she is still trying to make something of herself. She knows that Sister B is saying that just to show her up in front of company so Sister A is quite right when she calls Sister B an old cow and then brings up the fact that Sister B is grooming her daughters to be exactly like her, brainless ninnies who feel that they don't exist without a man. Sister A also reveals what really happened to Fluffy in 1974.

In this case, Sister A was absolutely right to deal with the issue in this way.

Stick To The Issue

If an argument arises, you must deal with the issue at hand. A family gathering is an emotional minefield; there are years and years of shared memories and resentment. It is far too easy to let a situation escalate. You must look at the issue singularly and rationally.

When Father says, "What have you done with your hair?" Sister A knows the issue is the loan for $2500 she has not repaid. She tells Father that it is just like him to ruin the entire day, that money has always been more important to him than his children's happiness, that she was virtually ignored by him as a child because of his pursuit for the mighty dollar. She brings up his affair with the Denny's waitress and tells him that thanks to him, she will never trust a man again.

Sister A was able to recognize the issue and address it immediately, and once again handled the situation correctly. It is not her fault if people cannot deal with an issue reasonably, when they were the ones who started it.

Set Limits

Your job as host is to make sure that the day passes smoothly. If you see tension or conflict on the horizon, it is your duty to nip it in the bud.

When Sister A hears Mother say, "Pass the peas," she knows that she is trying to take control of the event. She knows that Mother refuses to see that her little girl has grown up. Even though she has built a life of her own, she knows that she will never escape from that woman's toxic cloud, that if she doesn't break free she will be smothered. She tells Mother that she is sick of her butting in and furthermore, her past addiction to Contact C left the children feeling alone and abandoned. Sister A knocks over the dining room table and orders everyone out.

Sister A handled this situation splendidly. She was able to spot a potential problem and halt it before it got out of control.

Sister A will probably be spending Thanksgiving alone this year with a bottle of Chianti, a Lean Cuisine and a copy of the *Panic Room* and I, er...she just doesn't care. She is happy on her own and does not need these people. She will probably spend Christmas the same way unless someone apologizes and does it soon.

Using these tips, have a healthy, happy Thanksgiving! •*HW*•

Dos and Don'ts for Dating a Magician

By Christina Delia

AH, MEN. You might say that all men are magicians. Masters in the art of illusion, but capable of pulling bouquets of roses out of thin air when necessary.

If an enchanter is what you're after, follow these simple dos and don'ts, so that romance doesn't become a part of his disappearing act.

Do appreciate the little things

Nothing says fun like a rabbit in your hat...even if it means a few droppings in said French designer chapeau. A sophisticated female appreciates her wacky wizard for all of his worth.

Don't get put off by his wardrobe

Look at it as if he will always be ready for an impromptu costume party. There are many women who view a man in a cape and top hat as a mysterious, sexy sight to behold...or did you not see *Phantom of the Opera*?

Do perform tricks in bed

The lucky girl who bags a magician gets to have a trained performer on her hands. The best thing to do in a romantic situation is to loosen up by letting him tie you up, or if he's in the right mood, saw you in half. You should be blindfolded so as to truly enjoy all of the SENSATIONS that such an experience offers. If he insists that you, "pick a card, any card," consider it as extended foreplay.

Don't belabour the point

When choosing "Our Song", refrain from picking tunes that have "magic" in the title. *This Magic Moment, The Magic Touch*, and *He's a Magic Man* may seem ideal at the start of the affair, but will quickly lose their appeal. Many women eventually find themselves asking where the magic went, but keep their precious love songs intact. That is why there has never been a song called Son of a Sewage-Maintenance Man.

Do play the part of a lovely assistant

Any magician's foreign-born supermodel girlfriend will tell you, it's tough watching your man ravish a skimpily clad helper with his eighteen-inch swords.

Engaging in that sort of activity night after night may seem questionable, and could certainly take its toll on your relationship. The magic word here is trust. True, the bimbo in the box is very attractive, in a passing-craze, "now you see her, now you don't" sort of way. Just remember that you're the only one he'd ever truly take a stab at where it counts.

Don't interfere with his career goals

Maybe your guy's main aspiration is to be packed in a shipping crate for weeks on end, with his only rations being water and postage stamp glue. Listen Missy, just who are you to stand in his way of progress? Your sweetie has most likely been planning for this since the day he received his first magic kit and accidentally singed the hair from his Aunt Leslie's arms. As a direct result of the incident, Aunt Leslie stopped making electrolysis appointments, and your fella's career also took off.

Many women claim that their men swept them off of their feet, but how many can say that afterwards they found themselves shoeless, on a remote country road in Poughkeepsie?

Remember: the perfect anecdote to a humdrum life is letting a man with a wand turn you into a wife. •*HW*•

"A sophisticated female appreciates her wacky wizard for all of his worth..."

Plastic Surgery Tips from Jocelyne Wildenstein the "Cat Lady"
By Sharon Grehan

Thinking of having a little nip and tuck? In our little Q&A, Jocelyne Wildenstein provides some things to think about before surrendering to the surgeon's scalpel.

HW: Jocelyne, why do so many women decide to have plastic surgery?
JW: There are so many reasons; it is up to the individual I suppose. Some women have surgery to slow the march of time, some decide to go under the knife to correct a perceived flaw, and some decide to do it when their husband is threatening to not only leave them for a 21 year-old Russian model, but cut off their financial support, and the only way they can think to save the marriage is to turn themselves into a replica of his favourite jungle animal.

All very valid reasons, all very personal reasons.
HW: What if a woman can't afford plastic surgery - are there any alternatives you can suggest?
JW: Yes I recommend she develop a personality and learn to bake.
HW: How does one go about choosing the right surgeon?
JW: It depends on your needs of course, but there are a few things I've learned during my journey that I would like to share.

It is impossible to hold a medical degree from the University of Papaya as Papaya is not a country. You should never have to walk through a transmission shop to get to the clinic and avoid places that require a secret knock.

Clean, well-appointed premises are a good sign, and you can tell a lot about the surgeon by his clients. If the surgeon has a photograph of Mary Tyler Moore, Carol Burnett, or Michael Jackson in the lobby, you will know that he's a worker.
HW: Once I've found the right doctor, what then?
JW: Be specific about your needs and don't take no for an answer. Remember, like a house painter, a plastic surgeon works for you. Just as you wouldn't let a house painter say "No, I think it looks good now. I refuse to do any more work as it would be dangerous," you should not let a surgeon bully you. Make a clear list of what you want.

If they cannot deliver, tell them you will get someone else to do it. Then spread a rumour that he/she left a sponge behind your left ear.

Bring in a photograph, or a clipping from *National Geographic* as I did, to show the surgeon exactly the look you desire. Unless you have a knack for drawing, don't make the Joan Rivers mistake of handing in a sketch on a cocktail napkin.

Make sure you are going to get value for your money. Michelle Pfeiffer, Candice Bergen, Lauren Hutton are just three examples of women who were taken for thousands of dollars yet have very little to show for it. If the only comments you get after you've invested thousands are "My, you look rested," or "Did you get your hair cut?" then you have not received your money's worth. Would you spend $50,000 on a tune-up for your old car? No, you would get a brand new one. Same thing here.

HW: Any post-surgery tips?

JW: Well of course you must make sacrifices—I for one lost my peripheral vision after my last cheek implant but I weighed it over carefully and realized I only used it for driving so it was a decision I could live with.

You might be well advised during your convalescence to work up a few signals to replace the expressions you've lost in your face. (If the surgery is done right.) I twiddle the fingers on my left hand to show joy and use one finger on the right hand to express displeasure, but you will have many isolated weeks to find symbols that work for you.

Keep in mind that women are very jealous creatures. They will more than likely resent your transformation if they can't afford to do it themselves. My advice in this instance is to consider the source and do your best to rise above their pettiness. If it all gets too much for you always remember: nothing gives you a lift like a little collagen. •*HW*•

HW DISPATCH:

Woman Wins Case with "Distractive Eyebrow" Defense

A Los Angeles Superior Court judge dismissed reckless driving charges against a Malibu woman who slammed her Cadillac Escalade into a minivan full of semi-pro beach volleyball players last May. In issuing his decision, Judge Marvin Gardens said, "Having seen the plaintiff in my courtroom, I can understand how her eyebrows distracted the defendant so completely as to render her unable to control her vehicle."

The defendant, Margaret Dunwoody, had argued that the oncoming driver's hideously deformed eyebrows "mesmerized her," leading to the accident. The plaintiff's eyebrows looked "like a pair of bats taking flight," according to Dunwoody's testimony.

The judge concurred, stating he'd never seen such thin, badly-shaped eyebrows before. "In an effort to create a look currently popularized as 'sexy,' the plaintiff has overwaxed her brows to the point they've become a public menace. No human eyebrow should look like that," Gardens said in his twelve-page decision.

Bobbi St. Claire, testifying for the state, defended her depilatory abilities. "I wax my brows every other week and have worked very hard to sculpt them into an attention-getting shape, like Angelina Jolie's or Melanie Griffith's," she said in a breathy, little-girl voice. She then offered to show the judge her bikini wax, but he quickly declined. —*E. Hanes*

The Rules of Family: Advice from Donna Corleone
By Pamela Monk

DEAR MADRONE,
A good friend, who is a teacher, and a real stand up guy, runs a tight ship in his class and in his home. He has, however, a dead beat sister. Their mother does everything for her and nothing for him... that's another situation I could go into, but not now. The whole family is together at Thanksgiving, and the sister's kid bites my friend in the arm, so much so there's blood. My friend smacks the child, and reports to me that the mother AND the sister yell at him, and care nothing for his bloody arm. *Madonna!* Is this not a disgrace?? What can he do?
Astounded, Upstate.

Dear Upstate,
By the rules of family, you may not slap your sister's child without her permission. You may remove, gently, the teeth of said child from your arm, or the arms of your own children, but it is your sister's job to do the slapping, not yours. He only has three choices. Take it up with his sister, which is iffy, she is raising a brat who bites people and she doesn't see the problem. Or stop going to Thanksgiving dinners altogether, drastic but effective. Or let it pass, and blow off steam to his friends, who may listen sympathetically but under no circumstances should he say out loud that he genetically related to idiots.
God bless, Donna

Chapter Eleven – November

Lose 57 Pounds by Christmas!

By Elizabeth Hanes

FEELING BLUE BECAUSE you need to shed some weight fast or face attending the office holiday party in that tan polyester jumpsuit AGAIN because you can't fit into the slinky black slip dress you bought several sizes too small as an inducement to lose weight? Well fret no more! Don't let your chubby cheeks be immortalized in this year's Christmas pictures when you still have time to drop 10, 15 or even 50 pounds! With this amazing new weight loss plan, you can be as bony as a cocaine fiend within weeks—and do it without going hungry (or even using cocaine).

The secret to successful dieting lies in two things, says diet psychotherapist Juliet Lundgren: not depriving yourself and proper food combining. It's that simple! "Eat all you want, with foods combined from my three patented food groups, and you'll lose all the weight you want to," Dr. Lundgren says in her new book *The Sector Diet.*

Soap opera diva Therian Stokewater shed 20 pounds in two weeks on the plan, going from 105 to 85 pounds. "My show's wardrobe department was going crazy, 'Therian! Your hips are 9 inches smaller than you said they were. Now we have to alter all your costumes!' I was so excited, I couldn't stop grinning. I do have to be careful not to fall down, though."

Social climber Penelope Entwhistle, whom you've probably never heard of but that doesn't mean she's not better than you, dropped a whopping 40 pounds on the Sector Diet. "I'm embarrassed to admit I was once a size 10. But thanks to Dr. Lundgren and her sensational book, I'm now down to a size 0. And I feel great! Plus, not getting my period anymore is a huge bonus!"

So how did they do it? Dr. Lundgren graciously shares the basic plan with Happy Woman readers. Start today and by the end of December you'll have achieved that sunken-eyed, hollow-cheeked look you crave!

Rule 1: You can only eat the foods listed below.

Rule 2: You must choose at least one selection from each sector every time you eat.

Rule 3: You must eat whenever you're hungry, even if it's 27 times a day, in order to avoid feeling deprived and losing self-control.

Sector A: the Pale Group

Oatmeal, 1 cup, thin and/or overcooked

Parsnips, 2 medium, unpeeled and boiled*

Cabbage, 1 small, shredded and boiled*

Onions, white or yellow, 1 small, raw or boiled*

Lima (large, "butter") Beans, prepared from dry, 1 cup, boiled until mushy

Turnips, 1 medium, unpeeled and boiled*

Rutabaga, 1 medium, peeled and boiled*

Rice, plain, 1 cup, uncooked

Rice cakes, plain, 2 per serving

White Corn Tortilla Chips, stale, left in open container atop warm refrigerator, 3

per serving
Popcorn, plain, pre-packaged, stale, left in open container for several days, 8 kernels per serving.

Sector B: the More Colourful Group
Collards, 3 cups, fresh, boiled* 1 hour
Spinach, 3 cups, fresh or canned (if fresh, boiled* 1 hour)
Zucchini squash, 1 cup, fresh, steamed for 2 hours
Celery, 2 ribs, diced and boiled* until mushy
Iceberg lettuce, 1 small head, shredded and boiled*
Asparagus, 1 can, boiled* 30 minutes
Lemons, 1 medium
Beets, 2 medium, unpeeled and boiled*
Eggplant, 1 small, boiled*
*plus the water they're boiled in

Sector C: the Protein Group
Spam, regular or turkey, 1 can, uncooked
Anchovies, 1 tin
Sardines, 1 large tin
Potted Meat Product, 2 small cans, uncooked
Pig's Feet, pickled, 1 jar
Tripe, 1 pound fresh, well-boiled
Sweetbreads, 1 pound fresh, well-boiled

That's all there is to it! With all the choices practically made for you, it's certain you'll manage to stay on this diet. And with the wide range of foods to choose from on the plan, you'll never get bored. Look out size 0, here we come! •*HW*•

Sample Menus

Breakfast
From Sector A: Oatmeal
From Sector B: Beets
From Sector C: Spam

Lunch
From Sector A: Rutabaga
From Sector B: Collards
From Sector C: Tripe

Dinner
From Sector A: Rice From
Sector B: Lemons
From Sector C: Anchovies

Snack
From Sector A: Popcorn
From Sector B: Spinach
From Sector C: Potted Meat Product

Stalked by Santa, a Cautionary Tale about Dating Celebrities

By Elizabeth Hanes

NICK C. (NOT his real name) and I had only dated three times, so I was surprised when his obsession with me became apparent. I really go for older men, so Nick's warmth and grandfatherly nature had initially attracted me, but ultimately his significant weight problem and insistence on being accompanied everywhere by his midget entourage became turn-offs too large to overcome. It also hadn't helped when I'd discovered he was married.

I'd been a fan and admirer of Nick's since I was a little girl. I wrote him my first fan letter when I was, gosh, just five or six years old and wrote to him about once a year after that. Although he never wrote back, he'd always send me little presents on Christmas Day, which I thought was very considerate of him. Even though he showed me this attention, I believed in my heart-of-hearts that a big celebrity like Nick would never be seriously interested in a young girl like me from Truth-or-Consequences, New Mexico.

That's why it was like a fairy tale come true when Nick asked me out. I'd moved to Los Angeles to pursue an acting and modelling career, but I hadn't expected to meet any big celebrities right away. I was positively shocked when I saw Nick standing in the middle of the mall with children milling around him. I found myself staring open-mouthed and even dropped my Macy's shopping bags (you know, the kind with the little paper handles) to the floor in awe. I guess you could say I was a little star-struck!

Nick spotted me and motioned me over. I couldn't believe it! He whispered in my ear, "Whaddaya say we head over to Sunset for a shot of Jack?" I could barely stammer out, "Yes." He grinned and took my hand, which was trembling, and guided me outside.

I guess I half-expected him to have his sleigh, but actually he drove an 80s BMW. In the back seat were five midgets - the Elves! I felt as if I must be dreaming. First to meet Nick C., my childhood idol, and now to actually meet some of his elves. It was all too overwhelming for words.

We had a wonderful first date at Whiskey-A-Go-Go, and then Nick took me back to my place. The sex was great. Nick was very verbal and loved for me to sit on his lap and tell him all my desires. He grinned and said I was "very, very naughty." He seemed to like that in a girl. A gentle lover, Nick was tenderly responsive to my needs. His soft, white beard was like a love toy, and he certainly knew how to use it! On our second date, when he suggested bringing the Elves into the bedroom, though, I knew he was too kinky for my taste.

Still, I loved him. How could I help it? From the beginning, he showered me with little gifts. He almost always was jolly (except when he'd had a bit too much to drink). He was famous and rich.

Everywhere we went, people flocked up to him excitedly, asking to have their picture taken with him. I thought he was the ideal man.

"Nothing in our brief relationship would have caused me to think Nick would turn out to be a stalker."

Nothing in our brief relationship would have caused me to think Nick would turn out to be a stalker. We only argued a couple of times. He'd been hurt when I'd gently suggested he could stand to take off a few pounds and that maybe we could go clothes shopping together. I mean, his red-and-white uniform was cute, but it seemed like he had nothing else in his closet. He left in a huff that night, and it was the beginning of the end.

The next day, I received a strange phone call from a woman who only referred to herself as "the Mrs." and insisted she was Nick's wife. I was stunned! Kindly old Nick, married? I would have been heartbroken if I hadn't already decided he was too old and fat for me, anyway.

At dinner that evening, I informed Nick that I wanted to break up. Naturally, he demanded an explanation. I told him about the phone call and that I thought our age difference was too great. I mean, I was only 19, and he was at least … three times my age. Gently covering his hand with mine, I looked him in the eye and said softly, "Go back to your wife, Nick. She loves you very much." He was devastated. For my part, I couldn't believe I was breaking up with a major international celebrity.

We returned to my place for one more round of love-making, sort of a "farewell tour." It was phenomenal, as break-up sex often is. As we lay there in my queen size bed, each puffing a Marlboro Medium, Nick seemed to accept that our relationship was finished. We reminisced fondly about the three great dates we'd had together, and then he gathered up his suit, red longjohns, suspenders and cap, and was gone with a wink.

Within a week, I began receiving strange messages on my answering machine. Always anonymous, but obviously in Nick's voice, the messages said things like, "I see you when you're sleeping." Creepy! Soon, I began to notice him wherever I went. At the mall, I'd see him staring at me from his oversized chair in front of the mock gingerbread house. On the street, he'd be standing next to a red kettle, ringing a bell. At sporting events, concerts and in office buildings, I'd see him, and he'd be staring, always staring. Every time I turned around, there he was. Obviously, he was stalking me. Once, as I briskly walked past, I heard him mutter, "I'd like to stuff your stocking." It began to seriously unnerve me.

As Christmas Eve approached, I became increasingly tense. Before we broke up, Nick had promised me a "special visit" that night, and I was concerned he'd make good on his threat. In the end, I decided to spend the night at my friend Vicki's house, just to be safe. When I returned home on Christmas morning, I found a lump of coal under the tree. That's it. No card, no wrapping, no gift. A single lump of coal. Obviously, he'd managed to break into my apartment, and I was relieved I hadn't been there.

In the year since Nick and I broke up, I've managed to land some plum movie roles and modelling assignments. I mean, I've been on *V.I.P.* with Pamela Anderson, and I appeared in the new *Charlie's Angels* movie as one of the stunt butts. I've heard through the grapevine that Nick thinks I used him as a springboard to the big time, but nothing could be further from the truth. I know I'm talented. And blonde. And large-breasted.

I hadn't seen or spoken to Nick since our break up. At least, not until this past weekend. When Vicki and I went shopping at the mall, there he was again, just as I remembered him, sitting in his big chair in front of the mock gingerbread house. He didn't see me, thank goodness. I watched him for awhile and realized I was sad. Sad about what might have been. Still, I felt very glad I had that restraining order in my pocket. I think I'll go to Mexico for Christmas this year. •*HW*•

Do it Yourself! Paint Can Hats: The Perfect Xmas Present!

By Sharon Grehan

What you will need:

- Paint can (*cans* if making more than one)
- Paint
- Ribbon
- Glue
- Scissors

-It is recommended that you empty the paint cans first and give the inside a quick rinse.

-Peel off the label, and scrape off any excess paint.

-Remove the metal handle.

-Cut out the heads of children and relatives from your photo album.

-If you are right-handed it is best to put the scissors in the right hand and turn with the left.

-Reverse the process if you are left-handed.

-When you have cut out all of the photos lay them flat on a coffee table or any other flat surface (the floor is also very flat as is the kitchen table) make sure you have the photos facing up (toward you) or it won't make any sense.

-Place a photo against the paint can to determine where it should be positioned. Special Note: It will not stick because you have not used any glue. It may help to trace the photo (with a pencil or pen, not your finger) so you can remember positioning.

-Very carefully open the bottle of glue.

It will be very sticky. Place a small dab (about the size of a pea) on the back of the photo. (The back of the photo is the opposite of the image side). Try not to test the glue with your tongue as glue can be toxic.

-Gently place the photo on the paint can. It should stick. If the photo sticks to your hand, you have put the glue on the front of the photo and will have to start over. (Be sure to wash your hands.)

-When you have successfully glued a photo, repeat all the steps until the paint can is covered. (With photos)

-Allow the can to dry for 72 hours

-Attach a ribbon to the little holes at each side where the metal handle used to be.

-You will find that the ribbon is usually bigger than the holes, but don't give up. By a process known as *twisting*, the ribbon will actually become thinner.

-Insert one end into the hole. (You will have to tie it or it will slip back out). Then tie the ribbon to the other hole.

-Try the can on. If it keeps slipping over your eyes, that means it is too big and you will have to glue small pieces of foam to the sides. (Wait for the glue to dry before trying it on again). If the can is too small, then that means your head is far too big and that you will need a longer ribbon.

-Once the can has been sized, tie the ribbon (tying instructions available in our December 2003 issue in the article "Why Knot?"), admire yourself in the mirror and step out to drive the PTA green with envy!

•*HW*•

Twisting How-To

Hold the ribbon in your left hand and put the other end in your right hand pull it taut (the ribbon not your hand) and turn your right hand clockwise until the wrist bone forces you to stop. Then, turn the left hand counter-clockwise. Repeat until the ribbon is the desired width. (Reverse if you are left handed.)

Dream Your Way to Success!

By Elayne Chenoweth-Bugg as told to Elizabeth Hanes

WHATEVER YOUR GOAL for the new year, whether it's to lose 50 pounds or make $50,000, you can enhance your chances for success through dream interpretation. It's widely known that everyone dreams. But not everyone knows you can shape the course of your future by tuning in to your dreams and heeding the subliminal messages embedded within them.

Dream interpretation is an exacting science. And I should know: I'm a paranormal psychologist who wrote my doctoral dissertation on the subject. Now, in an act of charity, and to promote my forthcoming eBook on the subject, I share my life's work with you.

Here is an excerpt from*: Dream Your Way to Success in 30 Days or Less*

Through my exhaustive research, including casual interviews with acquaintances at cocktail parties, I've been able to identify the five most common dreams and their meanings. Put this information to good use and watch as your "dreams come true"!

Nudity: This usually represents an issue of nakedness, of feeling naked, of being naked. It could mean you have a pending doctor's appointment. Or perhaps this dream is saying you should pose for a Playboy pictorial. For nudists, the equivalent of this dream is to dream of being clothed while in a social situation. And for the record, people who sleep in the nude are no more likely to have nudity dreams than anyone else.

Falling: This probably means you have a drinking problem. Or an inner-ear infection. It could also mean autumn is your favorite time of year. Or that you have an irrational phobia of dead leaves. You may have watched too many episodes of *The Time Tunnel* as a youngster, or perhaps Hitchcock's *Vertigo* really freaked you out.

Teeth falling out: You need immediate dental work. You're a liar or a gossip. Or a politician. This dream could also mean there's something rotten in your life, perhaps a piece of soft fruit you forgot about in your briefcase. It may also indicate you're a rotten person who's best advised to move to another state and begin anew under an assumed name.

Being chased: This dream is rooted in childhood, stemming from a fear of playing *Pop Goes the Weasel.* It indicates you harbour strong anti-weasel feelings, while still perhaps secretly feeling that you are a weasel. This dream also commonly indicates a career change to being a cobbler.

Flying: This probably means you harbour feelings of being a superhero, of being superior. You think you're above everyone else. You can see everything so clearly, can't you, missy? Miss Harvard MBA. Miss "Mom always liked me better." Well, Mom is dead now, OK? Do you hear me? And she liked me equally as much as you. I know because she told me so. So you can just take your superiority complex and your six figure salary and stick it up your…

Dream Your Way to Success in 30 Days or Less is forthcoming from Quintillion Press. It will be available in the following eBook formats: PDF, PDA, PDQ, PCP, PPA, PTSD, PID, DPI, GNP, GDP, FAQ, Q&A. •*HW*•

"Two knives, two forks, two spoons, two glasses, two plates and one jar of Branston's pickle relish. Bill hated monotony."

Herstory: Meatloaf—A Love Story

By Sharon Grehan

Margaret Pearson wins a 2 for 1 appetizer coupon at Chucky's Honky Tonk valid Sunday - Tuesday for her tragic tale. Congrats Mags!

IT WAS A TUESDAY, that's for certain. Meatloaf. Meatloaf, carrots and Shirrif's potatoes au gratin, because Bill loved French food, Bird's custard with lemon zest, and fresh ground Folgers for dessert.

Bill's car pulled into the driveway at 5:07 and I finished laying the table. Two knives, two forks, two spoons, two glasses, two plates and one jar of Branston's pickle relish. Bill hated monotony.

He kissed the air next to my cheek as he sat down and I placed the food in front of him.

The meatloaf was dry, and I looked Bill to see if he noticed. He didn't. He looked up at me, smiled and winked. Winked.

I felt a surge of anger so great my hand trembled.

Twenty-one years of marriage, one thousand and ninety-two Tuesdays. If you subtract two weeks in Sherkston Shores every two years and accounting for three Christmases that fell on meatloaf day, that's one thousand, seven hundred and five meatloaf dinners. One thousand, seven hundred and five meatloaf dinners and five winks.

Five winks over a ten year period.

I looked across the table and looked at Bill's hands. They were spotlessly clean. Surgeon clean. I looked at the part in his hair, razor sharp and clean, very clean. No friendly flakes of psoriasis popping up to wave, just clean. His ears usually hiding behind thick brush were apparent and rosy.

Finally I noticed the cologne.

Bill continued eating contentedly as I planned his funeral. I would wear black of course, but no hat; hats are for movie stars and prostitutes. Reverend Postad would have to do, as Rev. MacIsaac was on holiday and the church's common room was still under renovation so we'd have to use the foyer but in my opinion it was just as nice.

I imagined for the last time what this one looked like. Blonde, probably, frowzy naturally. She would wear a hat of course and sob noisily at the back of the church. She might bring a friend to share in her drama of the unwed widow, but no. Too much attention for too little work. I would have a private service. Thirty-seven people. Seventeen from my side and twenty from his—after all, it was his funeral.

I rose from the table and removed the custard from the refrigerator. I made the coffee and added 12 Planter's Peanuts to the grinder. There were more dramatic ways of doing this, but why make a show of it? Thousands of people die from anaphylactic shock each year. Why shouldn't he? He didn't deserve an extraordinary death.

In the 43 minutes it took Bill to die, I cleared the table and washed the dishes. A funny thought occurred to me as I put away the pickle relish and Bill writhed around the floor gasping for breath.

I would never have to make meatloaf again.

I *hate* meatloaf. •*HW*•

Newly single Margaret Pearson

Offensive Driving: The Driving Style of Choice

By Elaine Langlois

"THE BEST DEFENSE is a good offense." This axiom of professional sports also applies to driving. Perhaps you are aware that there are styles of driving, just as there are styles of clothing and hair. Some are more desirable than others. Offensive driving is fast becoming the driving style of choice.

You have probably heard of defensive driving. This is a fairy-tale set of concepts peddled in driver-ed classes. Defensive drivers supposedly reduce the risk of accident by adjusting to the driving styles of other people, traffic, and road conditions. It should be apparent that this approach to life behind the wheel is incredibly passé. Why should we have to adjust to what other people do? It's they who should adjust to us!

Let's look at an example of defensive vs. offensive driving. Say you are coming down a ramp out of a hospital garage into a busy street. As you start down, another car starts up. There is no room to pass. The defensive driver would courteously back up to allow the other driver in. The offensive driver would force the other vehicle backwards into the traffic and proceed on her way. (Let us say as an aside that, if you happen to be going the same way as an ambulance with its lights flashing, you can follow it closely and really make some time.)

This example points up the modus operandi of the offensive driver. Your most precious commodity is time. Getting where you're going as quickly as possible is the only thing that matters. Some people might ask, is it worth risking your safety and that of others to arrive a few minutes earlier at K-mart? Of course it is! In life, the race is to the swift. And all those minutes you save by getting places more quickly add up. Who knows how many hours you may be adding to your life by becoming an offensive driver? Let's examine some offensive driving rules of the road:

- The maximum number of cars that can hurtle through a red light is five.
- Turn signals are for people who don't have anything better to do. Let other people figure out your intentions.
- Back out assertively. Do not look backwards or to the sides. You are a forward-looking person. Other people should just get out of your way.
- The defensive driver maintains a generous distance from other vehicles. The offensive driver stays just centimetres from the bumper of the car she's following. This can become a test of nerve and skill, particularly when 17 cars are rolling along in the high-speed lane and simply breathing on your brakes could cause a multi-car collision, something that can really ruin your day. Do not pass. Instead, intimidate the other driver into getting out of the way. Flashing your lights, swerving from side to side, and beeping the horn may help.

Do not use rude gestures, although it's OK for your kids to do so.

• Defensive drivers seem to think that special care should be taken when sharing the road with school buses. This depends, of course, on whether your own children are riding in them. Along the same lines, you should not feel any compunctions about cutting through slow-moving funeral processions and even tailgating the hearse. As Lily Tomlin said in *Nine to Five,* "He's dead. He doesn't mind."

• There has been a lot of high talk about the so-called dangers of cell-phone conversations while driving. Does this mean you should give up, while weaving through rush-hour traffic, discussing tomorrow's sales conference or Johnny's orthodontia? Should you perhaps pull over? Absolutely not! Talking on a cell phone while driving is no more dangerous than any other activity routinely engaged in by operators of motor vehicles, like reading a newspaper, fixing one's hair, or changing a diaper.

• Offensive drivers dislike the peremptory tone of traffic signs: *Yield. Speed Limit. Stop.* You should always proceed directly through a yield sign, as the other driver will almost surely "chicken out." The true speed limit is, of course, as fast as you can go without getting caught. When you come to an intersection controlled by stop signs, cross immediately, even if it isn't your turn. Taking turns is for losers.

• Defensive drivers use special care in night-time driving. Not offensive drivers. Simply turn on your high beams and proceed just as rapidly and recklessly you would in daylight. All will be well, although you may notice a few *faux pas* on the part of other drivers due to temporary blindness, as well as a little roadkill along the way.

• In any driving situation, stop and think: who is the most important person in this scenario? You, obviously. So put yourself and your priorities in the front seat, and drive on over the rights of other people. •*HW*•

"It should be apparent that this approach to life behind the wheel is incredibly passé."

The FAQS of Life

The Definitive Guide to Raising Your Children from Birth to Adolescence

By Crystal Click

THE TROUBLE WITH raising children is they don't come with instructions. The following is a quick reference to help solve you most difficult parenting challenges in one paragraph or less. (Because who has time to waste on kid stuff?)

1. I am so excited, we just found out we are having our first child! How can I best prepare for this new responsibility?

After a quick trip to the tent and awning for your new wardrobe, I would suggest obtaining a membership to a wholesale food warehouse. In the words of the famous Hawaiian Miss Universe, you will "eat everything in the whole world...Twice".

2. How can I teach my baby to sleep through the night?

This problem can commonly be attributed to allergies. When your child wakes during the night, wait for 20 or 30 minutes to see if the crying subsides. If she continues, bring her into a well lit room and check for nasal or eye drainage. Any visible moisture on the child's face is an obvious sign of allergies. A heavy dosing of Benadryl each night for the next 12 or 13 years should alleviate the symptoms.

3. How can I make my child eat Brussels spouts?

Egads, how can YOU eat Brussels sprouts?

4. When should I potty train my child?

I would say not before 3 or 4 years old. Before then they don't understand the potential harm in swallowing cleansers and disinfectants. If you are insistent on early training, perhaps swabbing out the potty with them the first time or two would be better than the old "learn by doing" method.

5. I am having trouble finding a reliable babysitter, do you have any helpful hints?

My dear, do you have a closet with a lock? Then all you will need is a simple bottle of water and cup of Cheerios for the very young, maybe peanut butter and jelly for older children. Please remember, safety is your foremost concern so please remove all plastic bags and cover any outlets with safety plugs.

6. My kids won't listen to me. How can I get them to do what I ask?

HOW ARE YOU ASKING THEM? ARE YOU YELLING? If the neighbours can't hear you across the alley, then your average eight year old won't be able to hear you across the table. Calm voices only confuse children. If you speak below a certain decibel, they can't discern between you and the television.

7. My son asked me about the birds and the bees yesterday, what do I tell him?

Obviously the lad is spending way too much time outdoors. Five minutes in front of a computer, television or video game should give him more than enough information.

8. My 10-year old daughter doesn't have any friends. She tells me the neighbourhood kids all make fun of her. I don't understand this because she has a wonderful personality, what can I do?

Your daughter is mostly likely suffering from a self-image problem. She sounds very self-absorbed. I would call a group meeting of all the neighbourhood children, sort of an open forum format. Put her in the middle and have the other children tell her what is wrong with her and why they don't like her. Then she can learn to focus on their needs and pleasing them.

9. My son is acting up at school, how do I get to the bottom of things?

First of all, the fact that you are aware of his misbehaviour tells me that you are way too available. If you work an extra hour or two in the evening, disconnect your cell phone and give the school a false address you won't have to worry about your son at all. Then your school officials will be able to raise him as they see fit.

10. What is a good age for my teenager to start dating?

What is a good age for you to start being a grandparent? •*HW*•

Antique Linens as Emergency Shrouds

By Elizabeth Hanes

AH, IT'S THAT TIME of year again: the holidays. And along with good food, festive decorations and presents, the holidays also bring family members. Lots and lots of family members. The old and the young, the large and the small, they all pilgrimage to your hospitable door because, let's face it, you're the only one in your family who can cook decently, decorate festively, and who actually had the drive to make something of herself in life and thereby possesses the wherewithal to give generous presents.

Of course, this annual influx of dozens of houseguests can only mean one thing: drinking. Lots and lots of drinking. Everything from traditional spiked eggnog to champagne to cooking sherry and vanilla extract. Wherever and whenever you can tipple, you will, out of self-defense. And so will everyone else, frankly. How else could you graciously ignore Great-Aunt Edna's habitual throat-clearing, Uncle Harvey's off-colour Santa jokes or little Bobby's incessant, bratty whining? Yes, it is alcohol that makes the holidays the warm and fuzzy family occasion we've come to know and love.

Some family members no doubt will overindulge, adding a little too much vodka to their eggnog or drinking the entire bottle of peppermint schnapps you had squirreled away in the freezer for a "special occasion." When this occurs, someone's going to end up passed out. This presents no problem for the perky hostess until one discovers that Great-Aunt Edna, having swiftly consumed a trio of snifters of cognac, no longer is snoring, or even breathing, and has not been for quite some time. You realize she is not simply passed out on the sofa but, rather, has permanently passed out. To put it delicately, she has passed away.

The obvious question now becomes: how do you decorate around Great-Aunt Edna so that the rest of you can enjoy your holiday festivities until the coroner's office arrives to transport her?

A couple of ideas spring to mind. You could, of course, simply throw an old drop-cloth over the top of her and let it go at that. However, since Great-Aunt Edna had no children of her own, was fabulously wealthy, and you were her favorite niece (who stands to inherit the whole kit and caboodle), your conscience might niggle you to do something a bit more classy for the old dame. If your conscience doesn't prod you, surely your desire to show off your superior breeding and impeccable taste in front of the rest of your family members will. Thus, I would suggest making a visit to the linen closet.

Antique linens make splendid emergency shrouds. In fact, the Egyptians used linen for mummification, a fact which might come in handy if, for example, you're forced to use your ostentatious, gas-guzzling Lincoln Navigator to run down a disgruntled ex-gardener who's somehow managed to slip past the security system into your heavily-guarded enclave. Simply toss his body into a brine pond for several days, fish him out, wind him tightly in an early-1920s hand-tatted standard sized bed sheet, roll him around in the dust a bit, leave him to cure in the hayloft for several weeks (in order to produce a convincing patina) and, voila! You have a sensational conversation piece for your library.

But I digress.

In the case of Great-Aunt Edna, no winding is required. I recommend you choose a festively-coloured antique damask tablecloth (but not one of the really expensive ones because, let's face it, you won't be getting this one back) in the general proportions of the dear departed. If she's tall and slender, a typical oblong tablecloth will do, and if she's shorter and more rotund then perhaps you should consider a large round. Drape the cloth casually over her body, allowing the natural softness of the cloth to create folds over the irregular contours. Depending on how the old gal is positioned, you might then consider placing a handmade pine wreath atop her head or torso area and adding a few coloured tapers or glass tree ornaments to complete the effect. Use your imagination.

As you await the whine of the ambulance sirens approaching to pick up the dear departed, you can relax, sip a cup of seriously spiked eggnog, and lead the family in a rousing chorus of Christmas carols knowing that, once again, you have averted what could have been a major decorating disaster. And that's just one more thing to celebrate during this holiday season. •*HW*•

HW DISPATCH: News for Happy Women

Widow comes clean after 40 years of lying.

Agnes Porter, 64, stunned friends and family yesterday by admitting she did not know where she was when Kennedy was shot.

Until this announcement, Porter had always maintained that she was attending an agricultural fair on November 22, 1963 when she heard the news of Kennedy's assassination.

"I think even at that time I was begging to be found out. After all, I'm not a farmer—what would I be doing at an agricultural fair? As time went on and no one questioned it, I started to believe the story myself."

Porter decided to set the record straight after her husband Rudy passed away in August. "I'm trying to clear the slate here so that I'll be able to be with my husband again."

Friends of Porter support her decision but refuse to play bridge with her. —*S. Grehan*

The Rules of Family - Advice from Donna Corleone

By Pamela Monk

DEAR MADRONE,

I have two daughters, such good girls, we share everything, I have no complaints, like lambs they are. But I can see trouble coming. One of them is such a glamour girl, takes after my side, thank God. The other is not a prize winner, sadly her face could stop a truck, just like her father, even though everyone will tell you that she also has his pleasant personality. Right now they're young, dates don't matter, but soon one will be getting all the calls, the other, nothing. It's harsh, but true. What will I tell the one when she asks me if it's her looks? I don't want to lie, but I don't want to make anyone unhappy. How can I answer her?

Honest from Park Slope

Dear Honest,
Under no circumstances should you repeat what you have just written to me to anyone EVER again, do you hear me? This is the only answer a mother can give a child who asks how they look: I am your mother, so you are beautiful to me. Memorize it. And mean it. If they want a real opinion, let them ask somebody else. Period end of paragraph.
God bless, Donna

Chapter Twelve – December

Herstory: Diary of Mrs. Claus

By Sharon Grehan

December 1

SAME THING EVERY year. I don't know why he insists on leaving everything until the last minute. It's certainly not as if they change the date each year. I get so sick of him running around in a panic. Perhaps if he spent a little less time golfing and a little more time working he wouldn't be in this predicament but he doesn't listen. Sometimes I feel invisible. I understand his career means everything to him but I think our marriage is starting to suffer.

My yoga classes at the YMCA are going very well. They also are offering a class called "Buns and Tums" that I might join.

December 3

I found a diet in *Good Housekeeping*, "Slim Down for the Season" and so far, so good. I've lost two pounds this week!

For dinner tonight I prepared a chef salad with a vinegar and lemon dressing. Nick finished it without a word of complaint and I was delighted but I should have known better.

In the middle of the night I heard stirring and there he was sitting in the dark, stuffing himself. Honestly! The man has no self-control. He polished off a can of cocktail sausages and half a jar of olives. I was so angry.

I am very concerned about him. He's very flushed and short of breath. I took out his suit and it looks like I'm going to have to let it out at least three inches!

He says it's muscle, which is fine if he plans to lift the presents with his stomach.

December 5

Nick hired two new elves today as management consultants and he is very excited. Balthazar and Roofie used to work at Keebler and are proponents of the "Force Field Analysis" technique. They've been studying the workshop all week and taking notes.

My muscles are aching but already I'm sure my bottom is firmer.

December 7

Well that's it. Rudolph just pawed through my flower bed. He has miles and miles of lichen around but he has to head straight for the tulips. It broke my heart to see all the bulbs uprooted. I confronted Rudolph and he denied it.

He is such a liar.

December 10

The mailman was quite nasty this morning as he unloaded the bags I distinctly heard him say "You folks ever hear of email?" Well, he can mutter all he wants but let's see his face when it's time to tip.

I had my colours done and I was shocked to find out I was an Autumn! All these years I was sure I was a Winter.

December 12

What with my yoga classes and my reading group I just don't seem to have the time this year to bake. Nick considers himself a connoisseur of cookies which is a big laugh because the only thing he is discerning about is quantity. I put Oreos out on a tray and he didn't even know the difference.

I'm thinking of getting contacts.

December 13

Tonight over dinner Nick seemed preoccupied. I asked him what was bothering him but he just grunted and said "nothing".

I wish he would share with me. He just shuts me out. When I try to get him to open up he says I just wouldn't understand. It's not fair.

I've lost 4 pounds! My smock definitely feels looser and I have much more energy.

I don't know what to get Nick for Christmas this year. What do you get for the man who makes everything?

December 14

Balthazar and Roofie's report has depressed Nick. According to their study Nick's management technique has been too autocratic. The pressure he applies each November/December does result in increased productivity but it upsets the equilibrium. They say he has to deal with the hostility and apathy he creates by concentrating more on the driving forces than the restraining forces. He has to start concentrating on long-term goals rather than short-term. Well it's all Greek to me but I do know that Nick can be very bossy.

Nick didn't react well to the report and stormed out to the workshop. He insisted the elves line up and demanded to know if they thought he was autocratic. The elves of course swore up and down that he was the perfect employer but I'm sure I saw a few of them smirk. It's hard to tell with elves though.

December 15

I got my hair frosted and bought a yellow sweater. Nick didn't notice.

December 16

We had a rather large argument after dinner. I tried to tell Nick that I need more. I need an equal partner. I told him that I just didn't feel important anymore and he flew off the handle.

He said I don't understand the pressure he is under, the demands that are made of him every year. He said I can't comprehend the stress that a man in his position has to deal with.

I was furious because it's always about him. His work, his career--what about me? I'm wasting away on the vine. There are things more important than a job and it's time he got his priorities in order.

He stomped off and sulked in the workshop and I ate an entire tube of marzipan.

Something has got to change. I think we need counselling.

December 17

Took a quiz in *Cosmo* and I think Nick is definitely suffering from a Saviour Complex. I left it out for him to see but he just laughed until his belly jiggled.

I'm thinking of taking a course in computers.

December 18

Dr. Phil was talking about conflict resolution. I wrote down a few of the tips and tried them out over dinner.

In a very calm manner I told Nick that I needed to feel that I was a part of his life. He surprised me by saying he needed my support. He said it wouldn't hurt if I took an interest in his business and I guess he does have a point. He agreed to go with me to a marriage counsellor in the new year which is terrific. Nick is definitely old school so I feel we've made progress.

December 19

What he says and what he means are two entirely different things. I made a suggestion today and he flew off the handle. I told him that since reindeers can only go 12-15 miles per hour if we got a Lincoln Navigator we'd have more time to spend together.

This led to a very long quarrel. He was astounded that I would want to lay off his "children." This upset me so. Although I try to bury it, I have to admit that I'm terribly bitter we didn't have children of our own.

Nick was trying so hard to make a name for himself in the early years and it did make sense to put off having children, but the time never seemed right and before we knew it was too late.

What's done is done I guess, but it really bothered me that he would think of those dirty smelly layabouts as his children.

December 20

Oh dear, this is terrible.

Nick fired Balthazar and Roofie today and the elves are in an uproar. He got rid of them because he thought they were trouble makers. He heard a rumour about the elves starting a union and I guess he panicked.

After he gave them their pink slips the elves went on strike and refused to work until he reinstates Balthazar and Roofie.

Nick took off in the sleigh and didn't come home for hours. I thought maybe I'd try to calm things down a bit and went out to the workshop with some cocoa. Emotions always run high at this time of year and usually a nice cup of hot chocolate and a sing-along clears the air but unfortunately the elves had been dipping into the cider. There was no point talking to them as they were quite rowdy and were getting very abusive.

Nick came home at 4 a.m. reeking of licorice. He was still pretty upset so I rubbed his feet and sang *I'm a Little Teapot* until he drifted off.

December 21

It is so strange. The quiet is deafening. No little hammers pounding, saws sawing, drills drilling. I thought it would be terrific to have Nick around during the holiday season but it isn't. He is so depressed. He just sits and puffs on his corn-cob pipe sighing heavily.

I tried to put a good face on it and told him that maybe this was a sign that he should retire. I told him with the money we'd save on postage and toys we'd be able to get a nice condo in Florida.

In all the centuries I've been with Nick I've never seen him so angry.

December 22

It can't go on like this; Nick won't even get out of bed. For all his flaws I do love him. He has always been a good provider and he has always been faithful. I can't stand to see him hurting so.

I'm taking control of this situation once and for all. I've invited the elves over for dinner tomorrow night and we are going to work this out if it takes all night.

December 23

Well the atmosphere at first was frosty to say the least. There was an eerie politeness throughout dinner. It made me very sad as I couldn't help but think of the boisterous times we've had in the past.

After dinner I asked the elves to state their grievances. Balthazar and Roofie had filled their heads with dreams of a world where toys came in as just-in-time modular sub-assemblies, a world where people worked 8 hours a day with two weeks off every year and a world where people didn't have to sleep in shelves with their coworkers.

Nick shook his head yelled "I'm not a millionaire!" and got up to leave. It looked like things were going to end there, until Simon, one of the more timid elves cleared his throat, shifted on his crutch and said, "I'd be happy with a surname, Sir."

The room went very quiet as Nick turned around and looked steadily at Simon. He put his finger beside his nose, thought for a moment and said slowly, "I don't think that would be a problem." From then on, the floor was opened up and they were able to come to an agreement.

It turns out they didn't want much more than a little respect. Nick was forced to acknowledge that perhaps he had let his end down, that he had taken them for granted. The meeting ended with a group hug and a toast to Christmas, then they all scurried off the workshop.

I was left with a sink full of dirty dishes but for once it didn't matter. It was worth it to hear Nick's hearty chortle.

I guess it's not so bad, we'll see a counsellor in the new year, work a few things out. Christmas will be over soon, so it will be less stressful. I've lost quite a bit of weight and look and feel better than I ever have. My computer course starts on the 5th and it sounds exciting.

Maybe next year will be different. •*HW*•

Beauty 911

By Elize Bergeron

Q: Elize, I have very, very thin lips. They still work fine and I don't seem to have any problems eating or kissing but I…

A: Please spare me the details.

I get asked this question so often I've devoted a whole column to it. I will say this once and once only. Consider it your Christmas present.

The only lips to have right now are the Angelina Jolie Model. I have very graciously provided a stencil and an easy to follow step by step list that will provide you with luscious lips for under $300.00.

(Note: You must use the cosmetics below or it will not work.)

The Angelina Jolie Lip How-To:

1. Scan and save the image digitally. If you don't know how, then I can't help you. Get someone without a manicure to show you.
2. Open the image in an image editing program and enlarge the stencil to 1¾" H x 2¼" W.
3. Cut around the line (scissors work best for this.)
4. Coat lip and surrounding area liberally with Almay Amazing Lasting Hypo-Allergenic Concealer SPF 6 until you cannot see where your lips begin and your face ends unless you open your mouth.
5. Apply La Prairie Cellular Lip Treatment Complex to the lip area and let the lips absorb the treatment for ten minutes.
6. Repeat once then go on to step 7.
7. Apply L'Oreal Air Wear Powder Foundation, SPF 17, Sand 40 all over face, avoid eyes and inside of mouth.
8. Position stencil ¾" below your nose. (Note: weak chinned ladies may find some overhang—if so, stop at the bottom of your chin and move splotch on step 16 up ¼".)
9. Using Chanel "Sienna" lip liner, follow inner line of stencil (Note: A steady hand is required. If you are a heavy drinker you may wish to dry-out before attempting this procedure.)
10. Fill in the entire lip area with one coat Revlon "Nude" matte liquid lip colour. (Note: It is very important to colour within the lines so you may wish to practice.)

11. Blot with Burt's Bees Wings of Love, Powdered Facial Tissues. Be very careful not to apply pressure and wait five minutes.

12. Repeat steps 10 & 11 and then skip to 13. otherwise you will never stop.

13. Coat center of lip leaving ¼" around with Body Shop Cranberry Spice Continual Lip Colour.

14. Blot with Kleenex Expressions, White Facial Tissue, Unscented using a one-two motion, do not exceed 12 pats.

15. Dab a ¼" splotch of the off white section of Almay Stay Smooth Beyond Powder Eyeshadow Shimmers in the center of bottom lip. (Note: As this must be exact, Dip pinky in shimmer, place your thumb in your ear, stick pinky out (of the same hand) and it should land in precisely in the center. If it doesn't your face is out of alignment and you may need to draw a grid.)

16. Apply two coats of Stila Lip polish in "Glaze" and you're done.

Reapply every two hours.

Q: I was at my local department store shopping for the holidays and I noticed a line of beautiful bags that the clerk explained were Fendi "knock-offs". I own a Fendi and couldn't find much difference--except of course the price. The genuine Fendi was $498.00 while the knock-off was $49.00. How does one tell the difference?

A: Dear Kathie Lee Gifford, you'll have to wake up earlier in the a.m. to fool me but to humour you and perhaps keep you from rushing out and recording a CD in despair, I will patiently explain the difference to you.

The Genuine Fendi: Is approx. 12" long x 8½" tall x 5" deep. The material is called Zucca and it features the FF logo pattern. The strap is made of dark brown leather, and is adjustable. Inside the purse, there is a small zippered pocket and inside the pocket there is a serial number printed on the material. The lining is marked in several places with a tiny stitching of the word FENDI. It comes complete with the store tags and the Fendi yellow dust bag.

The Fake Fendi: Is approx. 12" long x 8½" tall x 5" deep. The material is called Zuccata and it features the FF logo pattern. The strap is made of dark brown leather, and is adjustable. Inside the purse, there is a small zippered pocket and inside the pocket there is a serial number printed on the material. The lining is marked in several places with a tiny stitching of the word FENDI. It comes complete with the store tags, but no yellow dust bag.

Chalk and cheese. Now if this still isn't clear, perhaps Cassidy could explain it to you. •*HW*•

Knit 1 Backlist 4
By Julie Ward

HERE ARE SOME of the knitting books you might find prettily gift wrapped this holiday season:

Stockinette Stories

Twenty knitters, twenty points of view-this impressive collection of personal essays introduces the reader to those unique individuals who have devoted their lives to decorating the surfaces, walls, ceilings, and sometimes even floors of their home with knitted accessories. From the self-awareness of Nigel Cubby's no-nonsense essay, "You Say Tacky, I Say (Tea) Cozy," to the haunting questions raised by Maggie de Rainer's "Alone in My House" ("Why did my husband take the children and leave after I knitted the toilet tank cover in a red faux fur?" she wonders, challenging the reader to look beyond the obvious answer), to the exuberant, politically incorrect prose of Alyssa H. ("I made this alpaca and acrylic seashell mobile/I'd like to see you knit THAT, seashore!"), *Stockinette Stories* mines the rich vein of humanity in individuals who are often characterized as "scary" and needing to get "a life."

We All Loved Crafting While Talking Dirty So Much

The Wild Sex Kitten phone line inhabits that dark, edgy place where sex-talk-for-money meets the traditional needle arts. In this oral history, the authentic voices that emerge convey a slightly chaotic spirit and schizophrenic energy. After all, who is speaking—expert mistresses of sexual pleasure, or house-coated frumps who luxuriate in a job that pays them to sit, snack, knit, tat, and yap on the phone all day? The truth lies somewhere in between, and it is told by the women who are living it. Gradually, a picture emerges of dedicated multitaskers who have very high standards. This is best exemplified by one Chrissy6, who rants against a knitting colleague whose dropped stitch translates into coitus interruptus for her client. Includes patterns for three original projects:

- The official Wild Sex Kitten "pleasure script" for you to cross stitch, frame and hang near your own telephone
- A crazy quilt to construct from the lingerie that your stalker sends you
- A headset cozy to knit

The Lacy Poodle Lipstick Holder Project

In early 2001, thrift-shop owner Merrilee Briggs hoped to revive interest in French poodle dog kitsch. She put together several grants that allowed her to open her home to a diverse group of knitters. Encouraged by a steady harangue from Merrilee and margaritas from her Osterizer, the team knitted thousands of poodle-shaped lipstick holders in only 48 hours. *The Lacy Poodle Lipstick Holder Project* documents the weekend that changed ten knitters' lives, and actually killed three others. (The dedication of the book and companion video to the departed women is a touching reminder of that dodgy intersection where sociopathic employee motivational techniques meet old age. It also helped soften the jury's feelings toward Merrilee.) In the end, the Project suffered from the fact that Merrilee's vision could not be fully realized: she ran out of funding before the knitters could make and attach pompon tails to the lacy poodles. The unfortunate knitters bore witness as Merilee sold their unfinished handiwork to a surgical supply company and fled with the money. *The Lacy Poodle Lipstick Holder Project* reminds us that there are no easy answers to the important questions about how we choose to spend our time, the nature of greed, and whether your surgeon used knitted lace during your last knee operation.

Gonna Sell My Crap on eBay: A Story of Survival

In our increasingly genericized world where we're expected to buy more and more prefabricated objects, this story of a man who not only knits his own stuff but actually supports himself by selling it on eBay will inspire you. Readers of the survival genre already know Zane Stewart's work. He has recounted his previous tests of the limits of human endurance in *The Yes I Can Series: Sue Your Teacher!* and *The Lazybones Guide to Staying Healthy on a Daily Bus Ride Full of the Working Tubercular.*

As from his other books, the reader will receive vicarious thrills on almost every page, from the breathtaking description of how he piqued bidder interest in his signature piece, the "Single Colour Fair Isle," to the victorious ending, when Stewart discovers making a profit is as easy as inflating his shipping prices. Finally, *Gonna Sell My Crap on eBay* shows how the intensity of one man's life reaches new levels after he decides to make every decision matter, such as whether to ruin a non-paying bidder's life with trumped-up child pornography charges. Handwritten and hand stitched editions available. •*HW*•

Author Zane Stewart

Office Holiday Party Dos and Don'ts

By Elizabeth Hanes

EACH YEAR THE dilemma arrives wrapped as a colourful flyer adorned with crappy clip art, created by an overworked fellow employee who long ago ceased to care. It's the invitation to your company's holiday party.

All the office-advice gurus say attendance at the office holiday party is mandatory, not optional. After all, you've invested too much time and effort climbing the corporate ladder to risk looking tacky for snubbing the pathetic, grudging attempt your company makes once a year to look as if they appreciate you.

So how should you behave once you get there? This simple list of dos and don'ts will help you maximize your office party experience this holiday season.

- *Don't* bare your cleavage or wear suggestive clothing—unless your boss has previously shown a sexual interest in you AND you have a typed statement authorizing a 15% raise in salary for yourself, which you can get him to sign after he's had a little more to drink and gotten a gander of your silken orbs.
- *Don't* give a gag gift in the office gift exchange, unless it's a really hilarious looking sex toy.
- *Don't* drink until you're drunk. Your superiors will notice (and frown on) your repeated trips to the cash bar. Instead, do your drinking beforehand and show up already drunk.
- *Don't* gossip or get too personal in your conversations, unless you know for a fact that the frilly pink underpants you found in the boss's desk drawer really belong to him.
- *Do* take an interest in others, especially those you don't know well, by listening to their stories and trumping them with your own. Also, use this time to lecture co-workers you've never met before on how to solve all their department's problems.
- *Do* keep one hand free to offer a handshake. You can accomplish this by grasping your buffet plate, napkin and drink glass all in your left hand. Alternatively, you can balance your drink glass on top of your head.
- *Do* remain standing as much as possible, as it makes you look more approachable and demonstrates to your superiors that you're not falling-down drunk yet.
- *Do* bring plenty of rum or vodka to surreptitiously spike the eggnog bowl.
- *Do* conceal a tiny spy camera on your person to capture everyone's hilarious drunken antics for inclusion on the traditional "year in review" video shown to stockholders at the annual meeting.

Above all, remember: it may be an office event, but it's still a PARTY! Don't be afraid to let your hair down and show your wild side. The stockholders will thank you for it next spring. •*HW*•

The Twelve Minutes of Christmas

By Elizabeth Hanes

WHO HAS TIME for holidays anymore? And even if you did have time, would you really want to spend it with your surly children? Your alcoholic in-laws? Your toad of a husband?

Unfortunately, social mores still dictate that we do "something" for the holidays. But this needn't mean you must spend weeks, or even days, performing the traditional rituals of the season. In fact, in just twelve minutes, quicker than you can say "Merry Christmas!" you can have the whole season wrapped up and be on a plane for Barbados to pamper yourself throughout the remaining six days, eleven hours and 48 minutes of your Christmas vacation. (Note: this method can be easily adapted for the eight minutes of Chanukah or the seven minutes of Kwanzaa.)

Minute #1: Buy presents. Count up how many gifts you need and write the total on a piece of paper. Let's say it's 30. Point your browser to Amazon.com. Click on "Books" in the left-hand menu. Order the first 30 books you come across. So what if Grandma winds up with *HTML for the World Wide Web with XHTML and CSS*? Isn't she the one who always said, "It's not the gift, it's the thought that counts,"? Then let her put her money where her teeth used to be.

Minute #2: Wrap the gifts. In your Amazon shopping cart, for each book, check the "Add gift-wrap/note," box.

Minute #3: Decorate. Unroll an entire box of aluminum foil. Fold in half lengthwise. Make a series of cuts every ¼" from the edge towards the fold, ending ½" before the fold. Staple or tape these "icicles" along the top of the living room wall. Say "Merry Christmas."

Minute #4: Trim the tree. Place all lights, tinsel, construction paper chains, ornaments, and other traditional trimmings into a large box. Stand on a stepladder and pour the box contents over the top of the tree while someone rotates the tree on its trunk. Tie a Barbie doll to the top. If anyone objects, sneer at their taste and state cryptically, "If it's good enough for Martha, it's good enough for me."

Minute #5: Christmas letter. In your

> *"Unfortunately, social mores still dictate that we do "something" for the holidays."*

word processor, pull up last year's holiday letter. Change the date and the children's ages. No one reads those things, anyway, so no one will notice Larry had another liver transplant or Simone lost her front teeth over again.

Minute #6: Christmas cards. Announce your new commitment to the environment by mailing a single "chain" card. Include a copy of your Christmas card list and ask each recipient to cross off their own name before forwarding the card to the next recipient. Remind them to add fresh postage. Also remind them if anyone breaks the chain, they will be cursed for twelve days.

Minute #7: Go carolling. Crowd the family onto Junior's skateboard or Razor scooter, with Dad at the rear. Have dad push you down the sidewalk at break-neck speed, while the rest of you melodically scream *Deck the Halls* at your neighbours' houses on your way by. Watch out for the curb.

Minute #8: Cocktail party. Send email to all your business and social acquaintances, inviting them to a holiday cocktail party. With your husband posted at the back door, you greet party-goers at the front door, then direct them to the living room where one child will give them one hors d'ouevre and a pre-poured glass of wine in a festive plastic cup. Have another child guide them to the back door, where your husband will send them on their way with a hearty slap on the back and a "thanks for coming!"

Minute #9: Christmas dinner. Pick up the phone. Using your speed-dialer, connect to Pizza Hut, Quang's Chinese X-Press, or other favored food delivery outlet. Schedule delivery. If anyone complains about not getting a traditional turkey or ham dinner, remind them "there are children starving in Africa" who would be happy to be dining on Moo Goo Gai Pan, no matter the season.

Minute #10: Stuff stockings. Retrieve uncommonly used items from the medicine cabinet and junk drawer. Cotton balls, dried out permanent markers, and outdated NyQuil all make excellent "stocking stuffers."

Minute #11: Open presents. Gather up all the gifts and send everyone outside into the frosty winter air without a coat. Drop the gifts in a big pile and say no one can come back indoors until all the gifts have been opened. Lock the door.

Minute #12: Volunteer for charity. Sneak up behind a Salvation Army bell-ringer and push them to the ground. Wrest the bell from their hand while demanding that everyone within earshot to put money in the bucket, "or else." Continue for 60 seconds or until the mall policeman approaches. Drop the bell and run away. Feel good for "doing your part."

There you have it! You've accomplished all the requisite holiday activities in a minimal amount of time, thereby freeing up hours and hours to spend on the most important person on your holiday list: you. •*HW*•

Gadgets for Girls
By Elizabeth Hanes

IF YOU THINK only guys are gadget geeks, you need to get with the program, girl! Today's new generation of gadgets cater exclusively to the fairer sex. Here's a sampling of some things you might want to put on your holiday wish list.

Personal Digital Assistant with Ovulation Predictor: Dating just got a whole lot easier, thanks to the makers of the Blackberry. He wants to see you on Friday? You start to schedule the date, and whoops! Your PDA lets you know your eggs are ready to hatch that day. You suddenly "remember" you're going out of town on business for a week and reschedule. What could be easier? And just think: no more morning-after pills, no more nail biting in the days leading up to your start date, no more inconvenient pregnancies derailing your chances of making partner within three years.

Cellular Phone with Lie Detector: New from Samsung, this mobile phone can tell you instantly if he really means it when he signs off with, "Love you, babe." Built in circuits analyze his voice for signs of stress -- with 99% accuracy. You'll know when he's lying because the phone sends up a red flag (literally!) from the antenna whenever an untruth is detected. The feature can be deactivated for women who prefer to live in denial.

Robot Babysitter: She's not Rosie from the Jetsons, but she'll do a fine job watching your children while you're at a committee meeting or out on a date. Meet Gretchen, the latest in Honda's line of household robots. Designed to shepherd your children through homework, dinner, a bath and bedtime, Gretchen runs a tight ship. This no-nonsense robot is happy to hold your youngster on her 12-inch square plastic lap/tray table and recite a bedtime story, but children should watch out if they misbehave! Whining or recalcitrance will be met with a 20,000 volt, taser-like electrical shock, rendering the child blissfully unconscious so that Gretchen can gently transfer him or her to bed. What could be more charming? Pricey at $45,000, the babysitting robot is this year's must-have gift for the single social or corporate climber.

Thigh Driver: Why didn't we think of this? In time for Christmas from "As Seen on TV Products," the Thigh Driver attaches to your car's steering wheel. It not only acts as an exercise device, firming and toning your upper legs as you use them to steer, but it also frees up both your hands-allowing you to apply makeup with ease during the morning commute! Thigh Driver can be used alone or in conjunction with the Car-Curler, a curling iron that plugs into the cigarette lighter, and the Auto Spa, a 12-volt combination paraffin bath/steamer/aromatherapy module that fills your car with delightfully scented steam while providing a therapeutic paraffin dip for tired hands. *Warning: not to be used while car is in motion.*

Now, if only someone would invent a gadget that lets the men in our lives see what gifts we really want for the holidays, we'd be set. Oh well, maybe next year! •*HW*•

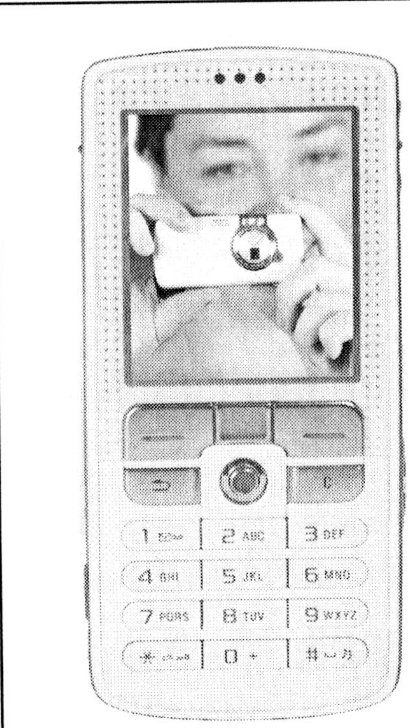

"If you think only guys are gadget geeks, you need to get with the program, girl!"

Random Acts of Malice

By Sharon Grehan

HOLIDAYS ARE A stressful time. In order to keep that happy smile pasted to your mug you need an outlet! Try one or two of these tips throughout the holidays and you are guaranteed to feel a whole lot better!

- Make it your business to not only tell children there isn't a Santa Claus but to express doubt as to whether there was even a Virginia.
- As your family digs into the Christmas feast tell them there's a prize for anyone who finds your partial plate.
- Ask the greeters at Wal-Mart where they know you from.
- Put a five dollar bill in the Salvation Army collection box and ask for $4.90 in change. Be specific. (i.e. 25 dimes, three nickels...)
- If you are having vegetarians over to dinner, add meat to the Ratatouille.
- Remove the labels from all the Christmas presents, and if you have time, from all your canned goods.
- When going through the department store checkout, ask the checkout person how much each item is just before they ring it through, then ask then how much that works out to per ounce.

- At the same checkout, present coupons after the bill has been totaled. Make sure the coupons are unrelated to anything you purchased.
- At the office party, introduce your spouse as your first husband.
- Whistle *Mademoiselle from Armentieres* softly during the Christmas service.
- Tell the kids Santa got electrocuted by a satellite, then murmur sadly, "If only Daddy hadn't used his cell phone."
- Ask people what their dream Christmas gift would be. Ask them to give you product codes, model numbers and info on where the gift can be purchased. Give them socks.
- On Christmas Eve, tell your kids that Santa wasn't fooling around with that "Better watch out" business.
- Spike the egg nog at children's Christmas parties.
- If someone asks you what you've been "up to," tell them. Start with the day after college.
- Buy self-help books such as *Managing Psychosis* or *Dealing with Dementia* and give them to your in-laws for Christmas.
- Butt in line, any line. •*HW*•

HW DISPATCH: News for Happy Women

Company Creates "Extreme" Jobs

In a bid to boost employee morale and cultivate a hipper image, stodgy investment banking firm Hamilton Hardway last week added the word "extreme" to every job title. "I kind of like it," commented Extreme Vice President in Charge of Finance Jake Robertson. "It makes me feel cool." This sentiment was echoed by Extreme Portfolio Investment Counselor Angela Dupree. "I love it! I really identify with it. It really sums up what I do." Not everyone at the company was thrilled, however. Extreme Janitorial Emergencies Supervisor Raymond Blacklock commented, "In janitorial emergencies, extreme is never good." —*E. Hanes*

The Rules of Family: Advice from Donna Corleone

By Pamela Monk

DEAR READERS,

I get tired of repeating myself, no one listens, but it can't be helped. Madrone, you keep asking me, what do you mean by family? My neighbor's cousin Dolly adopted a boy from one of those countries where terrible things happen…is that family? Or Sylvana treats her husband's aunt like it was her mother...is that right? Well, first let me say for me, family is blood. What can I say, in the village where my people came from, a stranger was someone you didn't have blood ties with, and we didn't marry strangers. Most people have eight great grandparents, I only have four. It's true, my hand to God.

All I can tell you who is MY family and don't try to tell me otherwise. Which is what I'm saying…no one can tell somebody else who is or isn't their family. Oh you can try, but it doesn't matter. It's beyond both your understanding and your power to change. But once it's decided, the rules are the rules. End of story. So now where were we? Oh…

A NOTE TO ANONYMOUS FROM THE NORTH SHORE

Under no circumstances should you serve the salad first, I don't care what they say about you. Where is your pride, and what do they know anyway about the way things are done? Salad is last, and please don't put the dressing on until you are just ready to serve. This will ensure the harmony that is now escaping you.

SHARON GREHAN, originally an improvisational comedian, trained at The Second City Toronto and has performed at all major and minor (very minor) comedy clubs in the city and surrounding areas. She has appeared in short films, television, provided voices for cartoons, and was a teacher at The Improv School. Her short fiction has appeared in various magazines and her column "Jenna's Diary" was serialized in *The Monitor.* Sharon is currently at work on her fourth book because she doesn't have time to do a second or third. She lives in Toronto with her husband Wynn and George and Lyle, professional cats.

ELIZABETH HANES holds a degree in creative writing from the University of New Mexico. She writes about art and antiques (hard to believe, eh?) for a variety of publications. She is also the long-suffering personal secretary of Savannah Lawless. (www.savannahsays.com). She resides in New Mexico with her husband, two faithful pooches and a pair of surly cats.

ELAINE LANGLOIS is a writer and editor and a native of New England.

PAMELA BONGIORNO MONK is a full time faculty member of Penn State University, where she teaches creative writing, both fiction and non fiction. She pursues freelance writing, authoring plays and feature articles. She has broken nearly as many rules of family as she has enforced.

JESSICA BECHT is resides in the state of Florida, where she has become quite intimate with election fiascos, hurricanes, and fire ants. When not shielding her alabaster complexion from the sun's brutal rays, she can be found strolling her baby about the neighborhood while silently mocking pink flamingo enthusiasts.

MIKE BOONE graduated from the Visual Language Interpreter Training program and published an article, "Interpreting: The Development of the Profession", in an alternative communication magazine. He went on to have humour pieces published in the likes of *Rampike* magazine and the *Knucklehead Press.* You can locate his screenplay parody in the March 1, 2004 issue of the online Ezine, *Fools Motley.* In 1998 he won first prize in the comedy category of the American Songwriting Competition. He's just finished his first book, Mike Boone's Guide to Dieting, a send up of diet/fitness books.

CRYSTAL CLICK: wife, writer, over-the-top mom, lives in a teeny-tiny house in rural Washington with her husband and five children. She took up writing because it was the only hobby she knew of that didn't take up floor space.

CHRISTINA DELIA holds a BFA in Writing for Film and Television from The University of The Arts in Philadelphia. She is a freelance writer of humourous essays, fiction, screenplays and poetry. Christina likes her problems rare and her men well done. She plans to one day join the legions of estrogen-happy writers who put the "ick" in Chick Lit, or even better, the "hick" in

Chick Lit! That said, Christina hopes that her yet-to-be released novel, *Sally Joe Puts Her Hoe Down (At The Hoedown)* will be a success.

STEPHEN JAMES'S past and current life can be summed up in five bullet points, of which two are just padding. He lives in London, which is a large town about fifteen miles from St. Alban's. He believes that most problems between men and women can be solved by sitting down at the piano and singing some show tunes. A traditional home-loving anarchist with an unnatural penchant for honey, he loves a challenge, but not a fight.

MEREDITH LITT lives in Connecticut with her equally sarcastic husband. She graduated from Quinnipiac University with a degree in English and is currently pursuing a career in publishing.

SUSAN SHOEMAKER a former flight instructor and air traffic controller, now spends most of her time looking for her car keys. She lives and writes in southern Wisconsin, but would much prefer to spend winters drinking and writing in the south of France. If you bothered to read this far, please contact all the publishers you know and tell them to send her money. Send it to her directly because since that incident involving the Fantasy Chippendale League, she no longer trusts the staff here at HW. Even though it was just a joke and she got her money back.

DIANE SOKOLOSKI earned a BA in music and BEd as an Artist in the Community. She has performed in children's theatre, political theatre, musical theatre, puppet shows, stand-up comedy and yes- as a street busker. Diane's writing credits include numerous magazines, including Toronto's *NOW* magazine and *The National Post.*

Diane had brief experiences as a police officer and a high school teacher, but her psychiatrist advises against talking about it. Diane is working on a children's book based on a true story about a skink who travelled across North America in a lunch box.

SARAH W. SZUCS is a writer of comedy and satire. She spends much of her time scribbling writing ideas on her never-ending list "Can I Quit My Day Job Now?" The rest of Sarah's time is spent as a Happy Woman somewhere in a rural part of the United States.

JULIE WARD lives with her husband and two sons in Austin, Texas. Her essays and short fiction have appeared in the *Austin American-Statesman*, the *Breckenridge American*, *Calliop*e and *New Delta Review.*

Random Acts of Malice: The Best of Happy Woman Magazine takes the women's magazine genre and twists it like a bleached blonde tress around a perm rod. With satirical articles spoofing relationship issues, do-it-yourself projects, and beauty tips, plus fake celebrity interviews, the book provides comic relief for women bored with the fluff offered by women's magazines in the guise of substance.

The project grew out of author Sharon Grehan's own dissatisfaction with the current crop of magazines targeting women. The final straw came when she found herself reading a women's magazine. After taking the compatibility quiz, the health assessment and skimming an article on female pattern baldness, she came across an article entitled "What Your Eyebrows Say about You," and thought "I can handle being unlovable, unfit and bald, but I will not have any facial hair talking bad about me behind my back…right in front of my face."

Determined to craft an edgy parody of women's magazines, Sharon launched the webzine www.happywomanmagazine.com in May 2000, to rave reviews. Elizabeth Hanes joined the Happy Woman staff in October, 2001, followed shortly after by Elaine Langlois. Grehan says without the tireless work, dedication and talent of these two women and the authors involved in the project, "It would be the Happy Woman Brochure."

Since its launch, the site has been reviewed and recommended by hundreds of media outlets and has entertained millions of people from all over the globe. With articles like "Raising Your Ungifted Child," "Giddy over Girdles!" and "The Sheep Shearer's Workout," the material appeals to women who love to laugh but really don't care what their eyebrows are saying about them.

Well, wasn't that fun? Perhaps you would also enjoy some of these other titles brought to you by Creative Guy Publishing/Liaison Press:

The Amityville House of Pancakes Omnibus, Vol 2:
ISBN 1-894953-30-4 – $14.95

AHOP features the works of four deranged, but really very nice, authors blazing trails into As if one suspect post-mortem breakfast trip wasn't enough, AHOP returns in its second annual volume to delight the sad souls who enjoy humorous speculative fiction. We can't promise AHOP 2 will be funnier than last year's edition, but we can promise that it will be greasier. AHOP 2 will again feature four novella length works from some of today's most ~~demented, twisted and depraved~~ creative and talented minds.

...

The Amityville House of Pancakes Omnibus, Vol 1:
ISBN 1-894953-26-6 – $13.95

AHOP features the works of four deranged, but really very nice, authors blazing trails into the somewhat suspect genre of humorous speculative fiction. This volume includes novellas from each author, so you do the math. Oh all right, four novellas, for one generous helping of 80,000 action-packed, hilarious words. Well, not all of the words are hilarious in and of themselves. But when you put them all together, oh boy!

...

Funnybones, by Paul Kane:
ISBN 1-894953-14-2 – $12.95

Paul Kane - author of *Alone (in the Dark)* and *Touching the Flame* - has returned, not to terrify this time, but to tickle the funnybone. Inside this book you'll find a collection of his most outrageous humorous horror, with stories ranging from "Dracula in Love" to "The Last Temptation of Alice Crump"...and not forgetting fan favourite "The Bones Brothers." Funnybones also includes several of the adventures of Dalton Quayle, that most famous of supernatural detectives. Before you can say, "Please for the love of God, no more, my belly," Master of the Farce Paul Kane will have you laughing out loud and embarrassing yourself on the bus. IMPORTANT: Do not read while drinking milk.

...

You're Not Very Important
ISBN 1-894953-20-7 – $13.95

Almost-Dr. Douglas Texter takes his readers on a whirlwind tour of the practice of self-betterment throughout the ages in this biting parody of self-help literature. He carefully explores the Big 12 myths of self-improvement, and at the same time, delivers a devastating, sardonic social and political commentary.

...

Titles available through the magic of the internet at the following fine, fine retailers:
AMAZON (US,UK,CDN) • BARNES&NOBLE • BORDERS • PROJECT PULP • CLARKESWORLD BOOKS • KAOSORB • CHAPTERS/INDIGO • SHOCKLINES • BOOKS-A-MILLION

www.creativeguypublishing.com

Printed in the United States
40085LVS00004B/41-64

9 781894 953320